STORY AND FAITH

STORY AND FAITH

in the biblical narrative

ULRICH SIMON

LONDON
SPCK

First published 1975
by the SPCK
Holy Trinity Church
Marylebone Road,
London NW1 4DU

Printed in Great Britain by
Northumberland Press Limited
Gateshead

SBN 281 02793 5 cloth
SBN 281 02843 5 paper

For Peter, George,
and the brethren of the
*Community of the
Glorious Ascension*

Contents

Introduction

Forms of faith are like shells on the sea-shore. Whether observed or not, there they lie, ready to be grasped by those who like them. Their number is innumerable, but only some take your fancy. They impress the eye by their shapes. None of them are alive unless you bring to them the spirit of life. Then, and only then, do they tell not only of the past but open a vista to the immensity of the ocean.

Forms of faith can be compared also to the jewels which reflect the light a thousand times for the eye that can see. But not all are precious stones. Forms of faith are like the stars. Some have shone and are now burnt out; others are only just reaching their peak. Forms of faith are spatial and temporal, but they reach out to the eternal beyond. They cause our hearts no rest until they find their rest in God.

The modern world abounds with forms which the ancient world did not know, and the ancient world used forms which are only partly used today. Many rituals, for example, are merely quaint, and even many verbal patterns tend to remain meaningless. Lists, genealogies, rubrics and the like remind us of discarded telephone directories. They neither evoke nor demand any response, let alone faith.

The Bible, however, is not a book of dead forms. The accusations and protestations, the denunciations and confessions, the laments and the thanksgivings, the curses and blessings, the taunt- and the love-songs, cannot fall on deaf ears in a world of continuing conflict, suffering, and passion. In this book, however, the attempt is made to demonstrate the forms of the *narrative* and the life which lies behind them. The narrative poses far greater problems than the forms of poetry. Where did it come from? What was it meant to do? Why was it handed on? How did it fare over the centuries? What does it mean today? Perhaps in no other field are form and content less separable.

Briefly the thesis of this book is as follows: The narrative emerged out of a certain conviction about life. This element of faith was always present, but it varied enormously, from place to place, from people to people, from author to author. Different forms of narrative derived from, and aimed at, different areas of faith. The reader must judge how, and to what extent, he responds to both. At a time when the 'simple story' is increasingly on the wane the task is difficult and rewarding.

My own view is positive. I believe that life without these forms of faith is meaningless. I also believe that the narrative is the basis of our culture and that without it we shall surrender to the repetitive clichés of mass media or to the chaotic flashes and meaningless signals of discontinuous sights. The narrative, and the faith associated with it, stands in direct opposition to cybernetic control and irrational, psychedelic jabs on our senses.

This essay is based on technical scholarship. My debt to the work of others in the field of biblical and linguistic studies is too great to be specified. After some hesitation I have decided to abandon footnotes almost entirely, since, once embarked upon, they would be longer than the text. This is one way of saying that the narrative often touches on the controversial. The expert will have no difficulty in spotting this.

In my select bibliography I have not listed the standard works, such as encyclopaedias and introductions and other handbooks on the Bible, such as commentaries. I merely mention the books which I consider particularly relevant to each subject and which the interested reader may also wish to consult. Some of these books fall outside the orbit of biblical scholarship. This is deliberate, for I am convinced that biblical studies must not proceed in artificial isolation. All the books in the bibliography refer to a whole host of other books—certainly enough to get on with in an area not short of sowers and reapers.

PART I

The biblical narrative

I *The Problem*

Stories told about people hold a prominent place among all forms of utterance. The biblical narrative, too, is probably better known and more popular than other types of biblical literature. Even if the original compilers did not intend to achieve this priority it cannot now be disputed. For the Jews the Law and the story of Israel have become inseparable. The book of Genesis sets the tone with stories which enshrine the nation's existence. Similarly the Christians have come to regard their four Gospels as normative for their belief. At their meetings and worship they recite and listen to readings from the story of Christ. Thus the narrative now outstrips all other forms to create and sustain faith. Hence it also poses now the severest test on faith.

This has not always been so. Until recently people loved the biblical narrative. They cherished the whole design and the wealth of detail. Nothing could emulate the direct response which all classes and races gave to the unfolding tale from Abraham to Paul. Other stories might also begin with 'Once upon a time', continue with 'And it came to pass', 'In the days of . . .', or 'After the death of . . .', but none achieved the unique distinction of warming the heart, feeding the mind, and creating a moral climate of conviction.

All narratives have one thing in common: they give verbal accounts of events which are alleged to have happened in the past. Yet the biblical narrative enjoyed an authority which tolerated no competition from stories about gods, fairies, and heroes. The Olympian gods, for example, might excite the reader's interest, but they did not present a challenge of truth. Less than a century ago Frazer could collect endless tales of demons and gods without destroying faith in the God of the Bible. But now this faith which is formed and informed by the biblical narrative has eroded. The greater our knowledge about the ancient Near East, often made available in sumptuous hand-books, the less powerful appears the authority of the narrative which fits into that framework.

This strange impact of scholarship cannot now be halted by an appeal to external authority. Gone are the days when the churches could and did decide the rule of faith based upon the accepted scriptures. Then the narratives shaped the monotheistic faith which the churches defended against error. With the aid of the canonical narrative they guarded the faithful against superstition and credulity. But this position of strength had weakened before, and has collapsed in, the twentieth century. Television, microfilms, and computers have undermined the authority of the narrative itself. How can tales from the past bear upon the present?

A narrative is as complex in structure as in the ways in which it is received. An audience may be bored or deeply stirred, and accurate reporting alone is no guarantee of success. Many narratives may interest but neither aim at, or succeed in, creating a conviction of any sort. Only when the hearer assumes that what has happened may, even in changed circumstances, happen again and affect him, will he give an assent to the story with something amounting to faith. However, in that case his interest shifts from the study of the events to the persons who order, or suffer from, them. The god, the king, or the hero, triumphed in the past, not because things were what they were, but because they acted as they did. The reading of the narrative will make available the power which in the past enabled men and women to subdue the world of events to their free action.

This kind of faith is, therefore, willed by the reader and listener. It cannot operate without a receptive heart and mind. Yet it is not uncritical, for it must discern false scents and distinguish between fact and fiction, or between the narrative which works and that which fails.

This critical function was not stressed in the past. As long as the Church acted with authority as censor the individual received the narrative mediated through the Church. In the absence of negative and hostile factors men responded to the stories of Patriarchs, Lawgivers, Heroes, Judges, Kings, Prophets, Priests, Psalmists, Scribes in the Old Testament, to Jesus, Disciples, Apostles, Evangelists in the New, as if they were happening here and now. Faith created experience, and experience confirmed faith. Whatever the vicissitudes of churches and nations the biblical narrative proved itself in the battle of life.

This monolithic faith has been worn away and can never again be restored. It is a loss which may lead to a greater gain, for the forms of faith, which correspond to the biblical narrative, shape a great variety of levels of experience. Their multiplicity demands a range of faith which goes beyond the simplistic understanding of events. The response to every type of narrative will have a specific quality. It will not be restricted to the area of happening alone, as if the 'it happened then'—'it happens now' dialectic were the only one. Instead we uncover the ancient well, layer by layer, so as to fill our empty bucket with the water of life. As we shall try to show, the event as such is only one ingredient in the formation of the narrative. Faith, too, operates in an immeasurably larger field.

2 *Ancient Near East*

The biblical stories cannot be understood in isolation from the traditions of the ancient Near East. From the time before Samuel to that after the Maccabees the Hebrews have recorded and told their stories within a common culture. Its wish and accomplishment to preserve events from oblivion may be traced back to the third millennium. From Egypt to the Persian Gulf the needs of the people were no longer met with speech, songs, and pictures alone. Their way of life and belief required the expression of permanence which only the art of writing could fulfil. Stories were not only told or painted but also transmitted and distributed.

The *Epic of Gilgamesh* provides the outstanding example. The Sumerian conquerors of Mesopotamia can still be detected behind this story. Their successful development of the indigenous culture, of irrigation schemes, and building projects with timber, as well as the inner tensions of government and society, are reflected in the exploits of Gilgamesh and his friend Enkidu. They fight, grapple with the bull, and court disaster through excess and arrogance. Enkidu dies and Gilgamesh finds the herb of immortality snatched from him by the serpent. The motifs of the ancient world are already voiced here; a later hand thought fit to incorporate the story of the Flood.

The purpose of this popular tale is clear. Those who tell it mean to affirm life, to promote fertility, and to secure power. Politically and economically speaking, this form of story creates the faith which moves the hearers to behave themselves well for the good of society. Yet it cannot be classed as an ideology or as cheap propaganda. Disgrace and defeat overcome the heroes. Thus a note of disenchantment lends a new dimension to the story. We sense the fragmentation of society and the wistful quest after the meaning of life. The narrative is neither triumph song nor lamentation. It is a prosaic account of life seen as a whole.

The Gilgamesh story does not appear in the Old Testament as such. Certain similarities, however, have been noted as between the ancient hero and Adam in Genesis and Samson in Judges, not to mention the much closer parallels which connect Noah with Utnapishtim, the old man of the Flood. These points of comparison are not in themselves very impressive. Yet the Gilgamesh form of the narrative helps us to understand the Hebraic purpose of transmitting the story of human life as seen through the acts of fallible men, for theirs is a range of success and failure which serves as a matrix for the disclosure of God.

A different type of story from the second millennium reaches us in the Ugaritic texts. These tablets are not only mutilated, but even their order is disputed. All the same a narrative with a propagandistic aim tells of the gods. Their intrigues, loves, copulations, sufferings, deaths, and conquests must have entertained the people of the ancient Venice of Syria; this city kingdom reflects its own history and institutions in the war of the gods. These epics are not primarily religious, recited at a shrine, nor composed for the court. The language is not lofty, the heroism not grand, the purpose not noble. The story is told realistically and at some length, as if the narrator were describing what he saw and recording what he heard. In this manner he brings the gods down to earth.

Ugarit transmits the form and substance of Baal religion, in which the 'upper' and the 'lower' world are united in action. When the hostile power in heaven is defeated rain falls on earth and the drought is ended. When Baal defeats Death (Mot) in the underworld the power of all living force sprouts on earth. The epic stems from the conviction that fertility is all and depends upon a power for which the hero-god must scheme and fight.

This pagan form of the suffering-dying-and rising god is physical through and through. The concrete event and not abstract ideas dominate the whole. Yet it opens up the perspective of another world behind that of man, so that what happens here and now has its counterpart there and then.

A long time before the religious forms of narrative the popular tale flourished in Egypt. Si-nuhe, for example, told his story not later than 1800 B.C. His is a success story, told by himself in the first person: 'I was an attendant ... I set out, came to, crossed over, reached etc.' He is always on the move until he marries an Asiatic princess and achieves a high position with plenty. He is a good father to his children, works for the good order of his adopted country, defends the weak, and defeats the enemy heroically. At length he accepts an invitation to return home so as to spend his last years in the country of his birth and to be buried there. He hands his property over to his children and sets out for his last journey. The courtiers welcome him, the king recognizes and receives him with honour and in his new high rank he educates the prince, while his necropolis is being prepared. Thus he rounds off a favourite's happy career.

The story of the two brothers, the adventures of Wen-Amon, and many others, display the same optimism in a world of trials. The secular story formalizes the individual's status and task. He masters events, shapes them to advance his cause, and gathers their harvest at death. Narrative and faith are allies to promote the good and enjoyable life.

The eruption of Mount Thera-Santorin north of Crete in the thirteenth century caused not only physical disaster in the area of the Eastern Mediterranean. The demoralization ended an era of confidence. In the ensuing dark ages the old stories were transmitted, but their ideology was shattered for centuries. When Homer and the rhapsodists sing again of Troy beaten to the ground, the aim is still life-affirming, but the story moves on a razor's edge. Fate governs the gods, the gods destroy men, and men are already their own executioners. Zeus, Hera, Apollo, Athene, Artemis, Ares, Poseidon, and the other gods, still rule in their own spheres, but we know them in their weakness. Homer evokes no faith in them as gods, but in the tragic fate which controls us all. The narrative inexorably demands still faith, but it is a faith in Athens and her institutions rather than in the Olympic pantheon. As Athens moves towards her peak atheism becomes a danger to be resisted. The ancient narratives are re-moulded so as to retain piety in an age when altars could be dispensed with. Aeschylus immortalizes the human dilemma of life in a world where the gods ordain and are appealed to and yet 'none from outside can help; we must ourselves cure our own case' (*Choephori* 470ff). Thus tragedy swallows up narrative to dramatize the greatness of Athens and to get the Athenians to face their problems. The tension within the narrative—Oedipus, Prometheus, Antigone, Achilles—has burst the forms of narrative. It can no longer be told as a sequence of events.

The Greek forms demonstrate how a creative society meets its needs by change. We can trace there an ever diminishing influence of religious belief. Tragedy, comedy, lyric poetry, heroic history, military history, personal history, dialogue, rhetoric, scientific description, pastoral and pretty romance: these come down to us with the great names—Sophocles, Euripides, Aristophanes, Sappho, Herodotus, Thucydides, Xenophon, Plato, Demosthenes, Aristotle, and lesser men. Their forms came to stay, but they did not aspire or turn out to be 'forms of faith'. In a way, they became the classical forms of belief in man, or man's attempt to come to terms with himself. The Greek narrative prepares the ground for secular history, and even after the decay of Athens, the triumph of Macedon, the chaos after Alexander's death, and the shift to Roman power, the verbalization of events and the transmission of historical records influenced the new world. Just as the Greek tongue survived into the Roman Empire so the making of history, realistic and propagandistic, flourished from Caesar onwards. Thus the Hebraic narrative, which had grown up a few hundred miles to the East, finally encountered and challenged another tradition. It shared with it a love for words, but it did not speak the same language about

God, man, and the universe. Hence the Christian story could at length attract the Greek-speaking world and thereby end its independent reign. In the last resort it was a battle of words.

3 *The Heroes*

The biblical narrative shares its background with the material of the ancient Near East. We breathe the same air, fight the same climate, eat the same food, live the same life in both. We detect aims, forms, and transmissions of stories which reflect the common origin. Egypt, Mesopotamia, and Ugarit precede the biblical narrators while Homer is roughly parallel with them. Their stories are told in the open air, recited at court, dictated to, and written down by, scribes, collected by editors. Yet the earliest stratum of all comes from before the time of a settled existence. The Hebrew narrative begins on a very small scale of moving Bedouin.

Very little remains of this stratum in unedited form. Yet despite the editors' work the book of Judges gives an uncensored glimpse of happenings during the conquest. The editors plainly state their disapproval of the belief and practice which they report. The adventures, treacheries, and outrages belong to a time when there was no king nor law in Israel (Judg. 21.25). We sense shades of Gilgamesh in the exploits and failings of these 'strong men', and the frequent allusion to Baal reminds us of the proximity of Ugarit. Jephthah sacrifices his daughter in circumstances similar to those in which Agamemnon offers Iphigenia to Artemis. Samson's strength, stupidity, and tragic end at Gaza recall not only the fate of mad Ajax, but also the exploits of Heracles. Radiant and long-haired he resembles the rising and the setting sun.

The story of Samson is perhaps the most intriguing, just because the divine presence is so strangely linked with the child, born to the barren woman, dedicated a Nazarite, pledged to abstain from alcohol and, perhaps, sex, long-haired and charismatic. The unscrupulous adventurer, trickster, firebrand, heroic extrovert, who is not only easily enticed but almost yields to

seduction with his own consent, is throughout the story a mirror
of God, a man moved by the spirit. This connection between
the Spirit and the episodic tale gives the whole a puzzling format.
The Spirit is not obvious as the divine afflatus, but has to be
discerned.

This discernment derives in the first place from the convincing
liveliness of the story. Samson, Delilah, the Philistines, vibrate
with detailed and yet sparse touches of original individuality.
The events are discontinuous, but Samson bridges the fragmentary actions. Yet the real continuity is provided by the
Spirit in Samson. Thus the story moves relentlessly forward to
its climax, when the blinded sun-hero is led into the hall for
sport. The catastrophe is the grand finale which vindicates everything that has gone before. Milton was right when he epitomized
the story's meaning with:

> Just are the ways of God,
> And justifiable to men ...

and declared that

> Nothing is here for tears, nothing to wail
> Or knock the breast

Samson's story transforms tragedy into triumph: the hero is
dead, but the spirit is alive.

The Hebrew sagas differ greatly from the heroic epics. Their
narratives are brief. They switch from one episode to another.
The judges are local figures in a disconnected sequence of events.
Only the god of the loose tribal confederation gives unity to
the fragmentary forces. He is Lord of battle, at the head of
his troops, thundering and blasting, testing and avenging, com-
municating in dreams, watching over birth and death. He is
the God of heroes, even if some of his heroes are little more than
gangsters. Behind Deborah and Barak, Gideon, Abimelech, lies
the portrayal of a God whom the narrative pictures only in a
perfunctory manner. The story-teller, unlike Homer, tells us
really very little about this great Unknown. He certainly has

not the face or character of the Baal of Ugarit. Just because the narrative takes us into the territory of Baal we note the absence of rival gods and goddesses. There is no intriguing for power nor a drama of succession, neither is the earth impregnated by the sky. The God of these stories has no part in orgiastic feasting nor in some rite of union. The description of outrages (e.g., Gen. 19; Judg. 19–21) does not involve him, for his presence is external to places, people, and events. Form and content of the heroic saga in the Bible are dominated by the strangely remote presence of YHWH. The name (perhaps Yah) stands for the fierce Spirit in these stories of aggression and defeat.

Subsequently tribal sanctuaries—such as Shiloh, Bethel, Hebron, Jerusalem—preserved these ancient memories of a God who acts not only as the tribal leader but also as all-seeing Lord. He is felt to be physically present, almost as the sun and the rain, yet he is not confined to one place. The stories convey a dialectic which no other form could so cogently bring out: the God who is concrete, earth-bound reality acts freely. The presence cannot be retained. Thus the stories prepare the ground for the conception of a personal God, who is not an abstract idea or symbol of configuration, but whose concrete presence can never be caught in picture, stone, or model. The heroic story does not elevate a super-hero to the status of divinity, but presents its heroic theme in such a manner that God stands over against the might of man. The foundation is given for the belief that only one Power, namely God, rules the world and that all power is derivative from him. The narrative makes room for a dimension of faith in which the hostility of the IT world can be met confidently with the help of the THOU. It makes Gideons and Samsons of the receptive listener who allows his fears and anxieties to be formed into an affirmation of life itself. This type of story was to have an incisive influence on the history of mankind.

4 God of the Fathers

Of innumerable sagas only a few anecdotal stories were destined to survive the many migrations. The conquest of the land of Palestine and the changing social order made them look antique. Yet even when Israel became a nation and kings ruled, the new story-tellers retold the ancient tales and wove them into their own creations. We now call their complete works by the name which they gave to the Deity and refer to the Elohist in the Northern, and the Yahwist in the Southern kingdom. But to what extent they represent schools or individual writers must remain unknown. Their aims concern us more directly and cannot easily be defined.

These story-tellers were of the Homeric age and shared the high cultural renaissance, even if they had not heard of Achilles and Hector, as is most likely. But, like Homer, they must connect the present with the past. The tales of the mighty men were not enough. Nor were they or their hearers satisfied with local humour and so-called aetiological legends which connected the names of places and persons with some sort of exploit. It is true that puns seem to have enjoyed some popularity and they are often preserved in the stories which connect with 'this day'. For example '... therefore the children of Israel do not eat the sinew ... on the hollow of the thigh unto this day' (Gen. 32.32), or, quite simply, 'he called that place Beer-sheba' (Gen. 21.31), which it remains until now. But the real task of the story-tellers went beyond a superficial connecting of shrines, fords, villages, hills, and customs with alleged events. They must create a convincing continuity between the present agricultural community and the shepherds of the past. They need a new dimension to bridge the gap of centuries. To do this they make a history of Israel which begins not only before the conquest but also before the stories of the heroes.

They did not have to invent the story material, for they received traditions of forefathers, whose names were well-known, even if they had left no records themselves. These forefathers had not been heroes, though one Abram is reputed to have fought with and against kings (Gen. 14). They differ altogether from their contemporaries, for they do not go out to hunt and they never stay in one place for long. Yet the patriarchal tradition places these men as leaders of dignity and strong authority. They are not in any sense aristocrats, but as they drive their substantial herds of cattle across the grazing-grounds and defend their right to water at disputed oases, they show themselves independent. The story-tellers accept their strange society without a word of explanation, and we, too, consent to the picture of semi-nomadic tent-dwellers and their families and servants.

Out of this store of floating and undated traditions the narrators take the material to form a family chronicle. But the sequence of clannish events about the Fathers is so loosely constructed that it can provide the earthly canvas to an unearthly faith. The form of the Patriarchal narrative is accordingly unique but by no means uniform. Indeed the variety is astonishing and at times the thread of continuity becomes so thin as to be almost lost. The story-teller alone guarantees that the continuity remains unbroken. He acts as the eye-witness who has seen everything he reports, even if, as in many stories, the narrative does not really admit of the presence of a reporter. He succeeds so well in this device that listener and reader tend to forget his mediation. The Patriarchal story exists almost before it is told.

The Abraham saga gives a new form to the travelogue of the ancient world. The dark father, who obeys a call, is not merely in search of better pastures but he is seen to move under divine inspiration. The story moves on the level of thumbnail sketches. The pilgrim's task remains obscure, his movements defy plotting, and the obstacles in his way evoke no heroic action but rather an almost passive acceptance of facts. The economy of the narrative militates against detailed description and full portrayal. Despite the anecdotal humour surrounding the birth of Isaac both Abraham and Sarah dwell in a solitude which the reader shares. The intensity of the clipped style dominates the form and reaches its climax in Genesis 22. The so-called sacrifice of Isaac can be understood as a reflection of the conflict between the generations, cultures, and even sexes. But this is to miss the true polemic, which concerns faith and obedience. The heart of the story is in a way its emptiness: the narrator has eschewed the pagan themes of the gods' loathing of men, man's usurpation of divinity, the earth's craving for blood, the slaughter of the child, the mother's protestation, the need for vengeance. There is a great silence in this story and no orgiastic climax. The substitution of the intended sacrifice by a ram caught in the thicket stands as the classical anti-climax. Abraham is not allowed to become a tragic hero.

The narrator blends several levels of narrative. He records as if he had been present, though the story clearly demonstrates that no one could have been present. He gives the word of dialogue in direct speech, as if he had been there to overhear them. He implies a divine presence, either by suggestion or bold citation, such as 'God said'. The narrative, therefore, moves on the secular level of observable events with dimensions of spiritual worth which cannot be measured. Thus the idyll of Genesis 24, in which Eliezer obtains Rebekah as Isaac's future wife, is a broadly conceived romance, which allows the transcendental element only to be apprehended in the leisurely progress of the meeting at the well. Gone is the clipped style and with it the sense of drama. Instead the form of the narrative favours the apprehension of detail. Yet the increasing material of human vignettes does not lessen the religious feeling of the whole. Even the later stories about Isaac, which concern themselves with domestic cares and wells, never lose the feeling of a divine Presence.

This richness of perspective stems only partly from the editorial success of mingling the sources. Certainly the Yahwist's directness, the Elohist's mystical aura, and the Priestly writer's sense of tradition and continuity, give the Patriarchal narrative a unique quality. For example, we see Jacob as the individual, the *homo religiosus*, and the tribal head. Yet there is more to this achievement than a mere mixture of styles.

The Jacob narrative is presented in a form of almost classical symmetry. The Patriarch's two encounters with God in Genesis 28 and 32 round off the chronicle, from the birth of the favoured twin, his strange youth, escape from brotherly vengeance after the stolen blessing, to the endurance of hardship and servitude among his own people, the courtship of Rachel with humiliation by, and ultimate triumph over, Laban. The man who returns to meet Esau, with Leah and Rachel and their children, flocks and servants, is a marked man, whose inner conflict corresponds to the outward wrestling at the ford Jabbok. Israel, the god-fighter, is born, not by tribal and social developments only, but by the narrative which sets them in the 'face of God'.

These stories are 'visitation' tales, because behind the fight for existence, the trance within, and the heavens above, the narrator places God. The Other is present in shelter, food, clothes, dread, and struggle. In conflict Jacob finds identity, not as a hero, but in the inexorable bond with the unknown. This unknown becomes known in a certain form, namely as One who sees, comes, and demands. The Jacob story assumes his absence in order to dramatize his presence. The narrator therefore discloses in the narrative the unexpected and free advent of One who is universally unknown and unknowable. The blind force which determines all life is now heard and felt, but not seen, as the Face, the Person, the Thou, which demands a free response to a free gift of Presence.

Yet the story material dominates theological polemics. Jacob's ordeal, centred on Bethel, focused on strife with brother, uncle, and children, beset by worry and sorrow, always points to God. Even episodes such as the rape of Jacob's daughter Dinah, the unwanted revenge on Shechem, and the ensuing misfortune, which show Jacob not only in physical but also in moral weakness, are milestones on a pilgrimage, in which human death also figures (Rebekah's nurse, then Rebekah, dies). Even Isaac's death is reported without pathos. The great emptiness—no human reactions, no supporting sub-plots, no real climax—communicates the hidden Presence. The listener, and later the reader, is Jacob, or, at least, a would-be Jacob.

This identification with the Patriarchs in the story seems to spring directly from the manner of its telling. It is at one and the same time positive and negative. Modern authors have rightly seized upon this almost terrifying character of the Patriarchal narrative as it has been handed down to us. Kierkegaard, for example, could find a mirror for his remarkable, and rightly famous, broken engagement to Regina by following Abraham to Mount Moriah. In a sense he feels himself to be Abraham: 'though Abraham arouses my admiration he at the same time appals me'. Again: 'In a certain sense there is nothing I can learn from Abraham but astonishment'. Is Abraham a murderer? Or a 'knight of faith'? He is not a tragic hero, for unlike Agamemnon, or even Jephthah, he is prepared to ruin the whole enterprise and promise of life. Now, however bizarre, Kierkegaard rightly discerns in the Patriarchal narrative the deep psychological fissure of man, the inescapable either-or of the human condition. In his *Fear and Trembling* of 1843, after centuries of silence, he re-opens the Patriarchal narrative to the existentialist bewilderment which frankly finds itself baffled by the story—'Abraham I do not understand'. A century later Thomas Mann in his momentous *Joseph and his Brothers* approaches the subject quite differently, but for him, too, Genesis, above all, is the narrative which ends mythology, or rather gives to political, economic, and psychological existence the *mythos* which transforms, through the story, the crass stupidity and wickedness of chaotic non-being into sustained, rational, and lasting being-and-becoming. Thus on the level of individual experience as well as on that of corporate responsibility the whole story discloses far more than its single components: from Abram's arrival at Haran down to Jacob's descent into Egypt a continuous map unfolds. Hence the story is not a patchwork quilt, however skilfully sewn together.

The Priestly editors bind into one sweep segments of these tribal traditions. The unity of the narrative not only links, from Abraham to Jacob, groups and generations of people, their household shrines and Gods, such as High, Dread, Mighty, their aspirations, fears, and triumphs, their occupation of various places (Hebron, Bethel), but, above all, a faith in One God. The whole narrative forms the faith and without it no such faith could be thought of. The God of the Fathers sends Abram on his mission into the unknown to fulfil the impossible promise to become the people of God. He who 'tests Abraham' is the same who arranges for Isaac to marry Rebekah, to dig wells and defend the treasured water, who favours Jacob at the expense of Esau, who fights with, or against, Jacob and lames him, who sets Joseph above his brethren and thus initiates the tragedy of the house of Jacob.

Thus the narrative spans the generations under a present, living, speaking, commanding, questioning God, who though invisible can be apprehended in visual experiences. He is not only spectator, but also direct agent. He is unquestioned male, without consort, active. He is concrete Being, appearing with a Face which may turn away. He is distinct, not to be confused with gods or demons, nor to be identified with dead heroes, nor a double or projection of tribal needs. The narrative goes beyond a story about gods or divine interventions and establishes a norm, namely of the God of the Fathers who is extra-temporal and extra-spatial in a temporal and spatial world. He is presented as Eternal in Israel, universal in the particular.

5 *The Wisdom story*

The descent into Egypt comes as a turning-point in the Patriarchal narrative. The narrator must leave the land as his hero
Joseph is carried away. It enables the story-teller to operate
with several levels of narrative. The theme of the clan, of father
and sons, of brothers in conflict, remains constant: the family
chronicle always hovers in the background. The Patriarchal
concern for continuity and the great seriousness of tone inspire
the redactor. Thus he deliberately interrupts the easy flow of his
story with the Judah-Tamar-Perez chapter (Gen. 38) as if to
remind his reader that the shifting scene to Egypt must not
obscure the importance of Canaan.

Nevertheless, the story of Joseph does build a bridge to something new. Canaanitish life must meet with the civilization of
Egypt. The form of writing accordingly forsakes the extreme
terseness of reporting. We may think of ourselves as lying on a
divan, listening with pleasure to a court novel. The factual and
the fictitious are interwoven, as in an Egyptian story. The
distance between ourselves and the events enables us to relax
with pleasure. We are certainly being entertained.

The Joseph saga strikes a noticeably secular note. This increases as the story proceeds, for at first, as the brothers conspire
against the favourite dreamer, and bring to their father untold
grief, we still feel the 'religious' Presence. The story implies,
though it does not cite, the judgement of the all-seeing God of
the Fathers. But once the victim is sold into Egypt these hints
diminish, except for Joseph's famous refusal of his master's wife.
His plea, given in the name of God against 'this sin', answers
to the grace and blessing which he carries everywhere with
him.

Joseph's God, however, is not the dark God of Bethel. The
story has nothing of the demonic-supernatural quality which we

associate with theophanies. Instead it makes room for a divine foresight and treats the whole world as God's court and realm. God rules all things as a celestial Pharaoh and his wisdom orders them in advance. Thus Joseph, who comes into this world from outside, is innocently charged, thrown into prison, and apparently forgotten, is in reality being tested and advanced. The divine Presence is in the whole and at every level of the story as it unfolds. The grace-and-prosperity aspect of God resides in Joseph's self-command, which, of course, also comprehends a rare ability to interpret dreams. Though God does not himself appear as a dramatic person, his spirit works in his chosen and makes of the dreamer an interpreter of dreams, and of the prisoner a high official of the court. The divine spirit orders lives and events, such as abundance and famine, so as to make all things come right for the chosen. The story is told in such a way that it secularizes the Deity in order to spiritualize history.

For the story-teller, therefore, a world of appearances, where men act blindly or wisely, in which a flux of events makes for fragmentation, acquires spiritual meaning through the God-inspired sustainer of life. When the miserable brothers appear at court Joseph refers them to this 'God' as theirs, though they had never heard of him (Gen. 43), but one feels that even after Joseph's self-disclosure they hardly accept the fact that they, the would-be murderers, had acted under and for 'God' (ch. 45). This new dimension seems to be even beyond old Israel as he is re-united to the whole house in Egypt and meets Pharaoh. He merely accepts it. Yet the God of Joseph is not given as an abstraction, like Iknaton's One or the irradiation of the sun, but as the Saviour and Reconciler of Israel. The Egyptian colouring of this ironical and symmetrically constructed story raises a host of problems only partly relevant to our purpose. Does the triumphant younger brother, the dreamer, the saving wise man, who defeats courtiers and keeps the dark woman at bay, the administrator, who turns a famine to prosperity, answer to any need in Israel? If he is not the actual physical link between the patriarchs and Moses, did Solomon's entertainers put him in their programme to further wisdom, or did post-exilic survivors of the catastrophe cherish the *Märchen* (novel) of the slave who had prospered in a foreign land?[1] Whatever the answer may be, the narrator concealed his tracks and in his non-polemical manner he simply concentrates on Joseph—without telling us if his Joseph is forefather of the tribe, contemporary with the tribe, or a nostalgic glance at the lost tribe. At any rate, Joseph is not a symbol or cipher, but embodiment of arrogance, suffering, growth, and responsibility, and these stages of the human condition are integrated in a story of reconciliation.

The form of the Joseph saga accomplishes a rare blending of materialism and metaphysics. In the foreground stands Joseph the provider, who seems almost remote and frigid apart from his dealings with his brothers and the ancient father. Behind him lies Egypt, the Nile, the Court, the long tradition and the people. Yet behind the land and its past God discloses his transcendent Being in the Becoming, the Providential cause of all events and dreams. The narrative does not confine the Deity to the past and present, but rather claims the future for him. Even the death of Jacob and of Joseph are but milestones on the long road towards the unknown future which is known only by God. The narrative shapes therefore a faith in the future, not with fanfares of assertion, but quietly and not without humour. This is not a form of narrative which we find often in the Bible. It cannot be made up artificially, for it comes from the deep experience of someone like Joseph. In Daniel and other apocalyptic tracts we hear echoes, and Luke takes up this form, among others, especially in the writing of Acts. The keynote remains the same: 'all things turn out for the best', for imprisonment and even death cannot impede the providential wisdom of God acting in history. This perspective of wisdom-behind-folly, of provi-

---

[1] Redford lists 23 items of Egyptian colouring, only to conclude that (a) the Hebrew writer 'was not so well acquainted with Egypt as has often been imagined'; (b) genuine Egyptian elements 'cannot be dated with any degree of likelihood before the seventh century'.

dence-behind-aimlessness, erects a vertical dimension over the flat horizontal line of mere events. The typical Wisdom story derives from, and then sustains, the Wisdom faith.

6 The Exodus tradition

The Moses tradition is created by a variety of forms. The heroic dimension of the Exodus comes after the neutral reports about political and social developments in Egypt, a very brief vignette of the child born, exposed, and rescued, an even shorter account of brawls in the streets, a pastoral scene in Midian, a visionary encounter with the God of the Fathers, a personal commission, an account of a demonic assault, and the long 'Let my people go' section of mounting tension of oppression and plagues. The different strata of narrative are woven into a consecutive story of liberation, rebellion, and vindication. The tone is secular, direct, non-mythical. The story-teller controls his material throughout, even when he includes songs and hymns. He chronicles every event as if it had happened before his eyes. Even the stupendous chapter 3 with its theological adumbration is treated with implicit directness as the story of a call. Detail and ornamentation are restricted to a minimum, but not wholly discarded. There is always a background sketched in, whether of brick kilns, tents, or desert and mountain. Light and darkness, drought and heat, famine and thirst as well as individual behaviour—the dancing Miriam, Moses's need for support etc.—give the stories a strongly earthly flavour. Yet this factual style not only accommodates the transcendental motif of the absent-present God, but tells the story in such a manner that the story is as much about Yahweh as about Moses. The priestly scribe shows his hand in chapter 6, where he subordinates the whole past to the present disclosure of the Lord. All the stories are shaped to achieve this faith, Moses and the Exodus being the focal point of God acting in events.

The form of the Moses narrative is unique. It may be compared to the many levels of the earth's stratification. The story proceeds chronologically, but it moves from stratum to stratum.

In this way its conception of deity abounds with a wealth which corresponds to that of the stories themselves. For example, the Yahweh who is said to ambush Moses at the end of chapter 4 bears a trace of the demonic-tribal. He is essentially hostile and his hostility is never wholly lost from the rest of the narrative. But the same Yahweh is also the God of the fathers who protects his people. The Midianite Yah adds the flavour of the ancient nature God, known in particular in fire and earthquake. Yet he does not oust the conception of the merciful God, but rather strengthens belief in Yahweh as compassionate and slow to anger. The two faces of Yahweh—hot, jealous, passionate, on the one hand; forgiving and generous on the other—are nevertheless brought under One Name. Without sacrificing the concrete conception of deity, the narrative in chapter 3 equates the God of 'this place' with the One who Is. Here the theological narrative comes to dominate all the other narratives, so that from now on the Lord of Moses can never be dissociated from the Name, which is 'I am', or 'I shall be'. The form of the narrative, however, maintains an air of mystery, an air of fear and trembling, so that the 'theological' stratum never turns into abstract dogmatism. The question 'What is his name?' remains a persistently haunting theme, unresolved and provocative.

After Exodus 20 the Moses narrative and legislation become inseparable. One hardly expects the story to be resumed at all. Yet after Numbers 10 the march of the Israelites is resumed in an even more dramatic narrative. The story of the great seditions enables the story-teller to develop the character of Moses. Miriam's and Aaron's death are duly registered, and problems of order and succession introduce a new element. The episode of Balak and Balaam is one of the strangest of all stories. The narrator uses anecdote and prophecy to reach the climax, namely the invasion of Canaan. His story ensures the continuity and validates the faith that the troops of Joshua were the grandchildren of the generation of slaves in Egypt. Thus the tension in our stratified narrative increases all the time. On the one hand we have legal principles and specific laws of a technical kind, brought under the heading of Moses the law-giver at Sinai, and on the other, we have the beginnings of a national ideology of the great march to freedom.

The effects of this stratification have proved lasting. Through this narrative the Mosaic faith is not only wedded to the Name and the Exodus, but also to a salvation history and to Law. The narrative has shaped the four-fold orientation that he, Yahweh, brought Israel out of Egypt so that they might enter the promised land so as to establish Law. Thus the original themes of Moses and the slaves have become part of a much larger whole.

Exodus and Promised Land become the matrix of biblical faith, whatever developments may take place in succeeding centuries. The somewhat bewildering story material, which is piled up in floating traditions and not always in recognizable order, feeds a deeply seated need. The religious mind, in its vast range from direct petitions to mystical mortification, orders the themes, which lead to the Exodus—guilt, panic, weakness, rebellion, catastrophe—and to the brink of the Promised Land—providence, miracle, vision, redemption, thanksgiving. The framework of faith is thus given by the story material, but it is the common mind which cherishes and transmits the framework. This tradition must be hailed as the watershed in story-telling, for from now on the *story becomes commandment*. The reading is not about Exodus and Promised Land: the indicative 'they went out' leads directly to the imperative 'Go out!' The Mosaic contribution to our civilization is, therefore, incisive, for it comes near to what is generally considered impossible and undesirable: the Mosaic story becomes Mosaic faith, or, to put it more generally, the fact, the IS, underpins and demands the value, or the OUGHT.

7 David

The survival of the desert tradition is one of the wonders of the world of letters. It may be compared to the continuity of the heroic epic of Greece. After the fall of Mycenae (*c.* 1100 B.C.) a dark period began. Yet by 900 B.C. Homer could celebrate again the victory over Troy (*c.* 1230 B.C.) and adapt the story to the demands of the newly stirring Ionian society. The creative moment had come when memories could be woven together. At the festivals of Poseidon and Apollo the rhapsodists recited for several days the glories of the past in order to enhance the vigour of the new. The epic retains the standard ingredients of narrative —for example, meals, landings from the sea, arming of men, funerals of the dead—to bring a heroic affirmation of the new society. In Israel similarly the story of Moses and the Exodus, of Sinai and the Law, of the rebellions and their punishment, gave the necessary backbone to the victors over the advanced Canaanitish civilization. The 'desert story' formed a militant ideology. From now on no history could proceed in Israel without an active identification with the past. To that end the art of writing was applied to fix the oral tradition. So far it had been found useful in the deposition of contracts, and 'memorials' in a scroll had been handed on (Exod. 17.14; Judg. 8.14). But now when Israel had its national shrines and feasts the occasions of public reading demanded more than sketchy injunctions. The time was ripe for literary compositions.

The immediate cause for the fusion of parallel as well as of contrasting sources in the book of Samuel must be found in the existence of kingship in Israel. The apologia for the alien institution rests upon a rich deposit of story material which is still anecdotal-heroic, as in Judges, but far more concentrated in the aim to which it is now put. Samuel and Saul, for example, exist in their own right, and the portrayal of the first king specially is surprisingly detailed and profound. From the beginning, i.e., the ill-fated search of his father's asses, to the end of the charismatic career, i.e. the consultation of the witch at Endor— was ever a last meal more touchingly summarized than in 1 Samuel 28?—Saul seems to take over power from Samuel and dominate the scene. But this illusory power is only the overture to the disclosure of the Lord's Anointed.

The formal structure of the apologia is new, not only in Israel, but in the Near East. For the first time, and with amazing success, different characters meet and the plot advances through the interplay of the forces they represent. Thus Samuel, Saul, Jonathan, and David and his men, act and re-act freely and unpredictably. Simple Davidic propaganda would have bulldozed the rough edges of the story. Instead, the genius who is here at work gives to everyone his dues. Saul, for example, impresses us as the man of the divine spirit whose desertion by God and possession by the evil spirit evokes the tragic dimension. It is in the complexity of human relationships, rendered truly questionable because Samuel, Saul, and David are themselves divided personalities, that the author must seek the only legitimacy of kingship which can be acknowledged by all.

This task became urgent under David. Before the kingdom was established the 'prophets' sang of Israel's glory and produced ecstasies wherever they went. But once David had united the tribes and chosen Jerusalem as the new capital the telling of the story became his responsibility. He decided not to drop the tradition of Exodus and Conquest, but rather to use it to buttress his own power. Many hands had a hand in shaping the narrative to this end. David's Jerusalem answered to Moses' Sinai. The past is echoed, rather than re-enacted.

The new themes are familiar to the regions of the Eastern Mediterranean. David fights with a lion as Heracles grapples with the bull and Theseus with the minotaur. David is God's darling like the favourite heroes in the Iliad. David mourns like Achilles. Though a king he displays the kind of melancholy which we know from Egyptian tales. Outward circumstances,

such as dew and rain, loom large, by their absence in adversity
and by their presence in the moment of vindication. Slings,
bows, arrows, spears, swords, and all the paraphernalia of the
warrior fill in the picture. Death serves as punishment, men
wallow in grief, and the exposure of the corpse is a disgrace.
Yahweh's anger scorches men's faults. We move in a well-known
world of antiquity. The war is not against Troy, but against
the Philistines; and the Presence of the Ark in which YHWH
dwells contrasts with the Olympic pantheon or the Palladium
which safeguards Troy.

Mention of the Ark reminds us of the freedom with which
sacred themes are treated in the new era. The 'Ark among the
Philistines' reads now almost as a burlesque, and one suspects
that the comic element, which is so strong in 1 Samuel 5–6, was
meant to contrast with the seriousness of the I-chabod tradition
of the fallen Shiloh (ch. 4). But tragic or comic, the whole story
reaches an unexpected climax in 2 Samuel 6, when David, the
ecstatic king, brings the dreaded object safely into Jerusalem.

The Davidic reign produced and furthered the chronicling of
events, and scribes were appointed to continue the collecting, and
writing, of history in a story form. Everything seems to serve for
the purpose, but eye-witnesses accounts provide the backbone of
the dynastic edification. David's entry into Jerusalem with the
ark, his matrimonial troubles, his military command, are closely
observed and reported. Here is a transcript of ordinary life, in
the fields, in the desert, at court, in the home, and with the
warriors. Never again shall we obtain a more vivid portrayal of
a shepherd, singer, outcast, warrior, friend, conqueror, king and
founder of a dynasty, lover and father, refugee from filial revolt,
disillusioned exile, ageing man, sick and cold, ready for death.
The narrator shows the whole man, with virtues and flaws
neatly balanced. Everything is subjected to the aim of completing
the portrait. The great elegies, as in 2 Samuel 1, are cited to flesh
out the character of the strange man, who does not welcome the
messenger who brings the news of Saul's death, who does not
gloat over the death of a hostile general, and who does not weep

and fast when his son has died. The sweet minstrel of Israel is
not a man of long speeches, and his great emotion at the rebel
Absalom's death pairs words down to the minimum: 'O my
son ... that I had died for you ...'.

Even when buttressed with lists of names from the royal
archives and decked out with specially composed psalms, this
story is hardly a political testament. If it came to be used later
on as propaganda or edification-history, not only in Israel but
also to impress foreigners, Solomon and his court may well have
had a hand in it. But even when the priests had done their best
by adding a quasi-liturgical cadence to the story, and when subsequent generations of courtiers, prophets, and wise men used
the story of David as a powerful tool to serve their own ends,
they could not falsify the original. Even when David's successors
embarked on disastrous courses and in a way discredited the
whole story of kingship, the belief in David of Bethlehem more
than survived. Even the physical end of the dynasty could not
crush the genuine form of Davidism. The archivists had not
copied in vain, for the records went into Exile, and there, in
Babylon, the Messianic hope was rekindled, the flame being
taken from the original torch. After the Exile the Chronicler
re-wrote the story of Davidic sovereignty, now seen clearly as
salvation-history under God. In the absence of king and kingdom the great hope fed on the past and laid its hold on the
future. The Davidic story had been written for kingship and the
Messianic faith answered to the tradition. The New Testament
is only one document among many which testifies to the lively
and problematic vigour of the theme of the Throne of David.
For nearly a millennium the figure of the shepherd king had
aroused a universal expectation.

The succession narrative bursts the immediate confines of its
own reporting. It creates a dimension of faith which believes in
sovereignty, in brotherhood, in charisma, in short in utopia. This
faith is a blend of personal yearning and public life, both
heightened to perfection. The narrative spans the centuries with
an overarching continuity of one David, a highly individualized

character, who becomes the focus of the love and devotion which he, during his years of success and failure, manifested for his God. The form of faith which corresponds to the story of the son of Jesse blends ecstasy with historical realism.

8 Prophecy and Protest

While kings ruled in Israel and Judah another radical transformation of narrative occurred. The prophets had always practised the art of telling stories. In their guilds they competed not only in charismatic acts, such as miracles, but also in the art of recital. At the cultic centres they had developed a function of their own, though still connected with priesthood. There Samuel, Elijah, and Elisha became heroic figures, especially in connection with the battle against Baal and Canaanitish customs. The memory of these great leaders was kept alive in story form, which incorporated traditional motifs concerning rain, fire, oil, corn, childbirth, healing, resurrection, and ascent to heaven. The stories of Elijah and Elisha commemorate the victory of prophecy over paganism. Thus 1 Kings 18 is far more than mere reportage of what happened during the contest at Mount Carmel but a realistic cultic saga of the contests between the minority, Yahweh-prophetic militants, and the majority, conservative Baalists. The story is wholly unlike the Ugaritic stories of war. The tone is deliberately prosaic and at times anti-heroic. In the provocative middle section about the ineffective absentee Baal Elijah is made to use offensively satirical language. Thus the typical prophetic story is shaped: realistic, aggressive, entertaining, successful. The pattern never fails even in connection with ordinary incidents, such as starving widows and sick children and lost property. These miracle stories become protest literature against the tyrannous, immoral, self-indulgent class. They reflect the revolutionary struggle against foreign influences, such as Queen Jezebel, and royal claims, such as Ahab's plans of private expansion.

The partisan fanaticism of the 'sons of the prophets' does not explain, but is nevertheless crucial to an understanding of, these stories in which the 'miracle' acts as climax and claim to authority. In these stories the social unrest and political struggle are firmly controlled by a divine Presence which acts contrary to the expected norm. The God of Israel is now experienced through the acts of the prophetic power, and this momentous No to kings and military rulers seeks a dynamic form of story, which is the brief, thoroughly realistic sketch whose climax runs counter to expectation. The prophetic guilds are not content with dramatic narrative, for their enthusiastic vision sees not only the enemy routed but their God vindicated in strange actions. They recite and transmit the form of *Midrash*, for it is in this *recital* of saga that they find the only adequate portrayal of a critical battle. The historical event cannot be 'searched out' apart from the spirit or word, which gave and gives life to it. The miraculous element is, therefore, in this type of prophetic narrative a kind of diapason which sounds in deep notes through the jarring cacophony of violence and human oppression. No wonder it is heard with even louder dimension when the New Testament resumes the story of the Prophet from Nazareth.

The form of the miracle story determines the content. It is, therefore, idle to introduce such questions as the evidential value of biblical miracles. Categories such as degrees of probability or possibility only obscure the basic sound of the theme, since nothing could be more remote from scientific observation. The prophetic guilds simply cherished the unknowable power through which all things interact. Later wise men tried to retain the notion of miracle as part of the rational and immanent power of God, which orders all things, but this extension of the theme leads to a philosophy of design and providence quite alien to the original form. The 'Holy War' atmosphere lasted only for a short time, and as the enthusiasm waned with the dawn of prophetic victory, these stories came to look like reports of conjuring tricks. As long as Elijah remains the centre of action, and Elisha controls political and military upheavals in the role of a hero, we remain outside the orbit of fairy stories. But whether the stories appeal to superstition or faith remains an open question to the end.

When the prophetic protest reached its creative climax these stories strangely vanish or fail to be transmitted. Very little narrative material remains of the great eighth century prophets. Amos, Hosea, Micah, and Isaiah identify themselves with the Word, and their message takes the place of the narrative proper. Autobiographical 'I' sections mingle with reportage about the prophet. What he has seen, heard, dreamt, done, and suffered now becomes part of the narrative. Amos verbalizes what God has shown him (ch. 7–end); Isaiah describes his presence in the divine court (ch. 6); Hosea narrates a brief glimpse of his marriage (ch. 3) which figures also in an impersonal account earlier on. But these personal marginalia are incidental to the message. Later, as the fall of Jerusalem draws nearer, the prophets' individuality becomes a little more prominent, but there is no real change of style. Jeremiah and Ezekiel sit at home, dictate, perhaps write, blending autobiography with narrative and oracles. Jeremiah, for example, scatters his plaints throughout, vocalizes his prayers, reports his symbolic actions, such as the purchase of a field. Similarly the younger Ezekiel records not only his call and visionary experiences but also symbolic actions or the symbolic interpretation of tragic events, such as his wife's death. The prophetic narrative is fed and enriched by experiences, but everything is subordinated to the message.

Despite their attack on the established order the prophetic form of utterance ceased to be purely revolutionary. The prophets took their stand by the covenant and they attacked the un-faith of kingship and cultus. Their critique of the present derived from their evaluation of the past. Far from deriding tradition they spoke in the spirit of Moses and Sinai. They 'reminded' Israel of the acts of God. Prophetic narrative becomes part of the 'knowledge of God', the religious tradition which must be preached, written, and transmitted. The high-water mark of detailed and entertaining story-telling will never be reached again, for when tradition comes to master events and experiences, the temptation becomes irresistible to tell us what ought to have happened, rather than what really happened.

The classical prophetic narrative testifies to a vigorous faith which stands over against vague generalities. Its strength lies in its prosaic directness, with emphasis on action and men's involvement in the action. The fall of Jerusalem in 586 B.C. understandably undermined the confidence of prophetic positivism. The tragic tale of Jeremiah sounds the knell to the direct portrayal of God's mighty acts. The transition from spontaneous storytelling to rhetoric is about to be made. The great prophetic ideals, such as righteousness, fidelity, holiness, and humility, always defied, and always will defy, their natural portrayal in story-form. Yet, as will be seen, they also created a powerful expectation and fed the Messianic utopianism. A child was yet to be born, perfect and gracious, the God-with-us. The story is outlined as a promise.

9 *Hear, O Israel . . .*

Ironically salvation-history becomes formalized just when salvation itself has failed to take place. The fall of Israel in 722 and of Judah in 586 B.C. produced a work of salvation-history, namely Deuteronomy and the Deuteronomic revision of the past chronicles. Fortunately the editing did not brush aside the legacy from the past altogether. The fresh spontaneity of the Samuel and David collections was not destroyed by the editorial framework. But in Deuteronomy 1-12, for example, the preached salvation-history can be heard by itself. The sonorous and repetitive style of this paranesis cannot fail to impress, but it does not enhance the interest of the narrative. Indeed, it is almost difficult to comprehend what is going on. The events are pushed into the background, for the preacher's concern is, of course, to moralize for the present: 'Know therefore this day . . . consider in thy heart . . . therefore thou shalt keep his statutes . . . that thou mayest prosper, etc.' The pilgrim people are not meant to 'enjoy' tales from the past but to heed the moral challenge. The narrative is shaped in such a way that the listeners are faced with death and disaster on the one hand, life and bliss on the other. The choice is theirs, history will be their judge, and God judges in history. The past does not articulate an inexorable fate but the possibility of a free response to God. Bondage, exodus, liberation, miracles, conquest, and purges etc. are not narrated for their own sakes, but because they converge upon the present corporate decision, which reflects the whole moral order. The story serves this ethos, condemns the evil and approves the good.

This type of history was to become normative in Israel. It looked back to the ancient type of covenant narrative. Then rulers concluded agreements with other rulers or with their vassals. They recalled the past as a legal background, as the 'whereas' stipulation of the actual substance of the contract, just as companies sketch their past activities nowadays to raise money in the market. But the salvation-history completely outgrows the simple stipulation, both in length and content. In the Deuteronomic narrative God himself is the maker of the covenant and the story of past salvations evidences his continual presence. Thus the Name of God and the story are not incidental to the present agreement, but God meets his people in the recital of the story. The narrative is on the way towards becoming dogma.

Yet despite this formalization of the story we can still detect in it prophetic teaching. Though it eschews the golden diction of the eighth century prophets and shows no trace of the spontaneity and even eccentricity of prophetic utterances, the narrative embodies the prophetic ideal of One God, One People, One Way of Life, and One sanctuary for worship. The narrative is unthinkable apart from the prophetic ideology and intolerance of pagan sensualism. It sanctions the ethics of monotheism and demands compliance with its laws. It is a narrative which identifies faith with obedience. It subordinates cultic institutions, kingship and Messianism, individual hopes and ordeals, to the credal *Shema Israel—Hear, O Israel* (Deut. 6.4–5). The story authenticates the divine demand.

The interplay between the story and the moral to be learnt from the story leads to great complexity. For example, it is now no longer possible to extricate from the second half of Jeremiah even the outline of 'what really happened'. There are blocks of tradition: namely, that in the face of the Babylonian onslaught the people must submit, that life in Judah may still be possible, that escape to Egypt leads to total disaster. Within this course of general events the prophet, too, appears in a history of testimony and suffering, in which, like Joseph, he survives in a waterless pit and deserted by friends. But whether Jeremiah had any dealings with Gendaliah, the temporary leader at Mizpah, or how the final stages of the disaster are to be connected, the narrator no longer seems to know. Thus we retain vignettes of great liveliness—none more so than the burning of the original roll in chapter 36 and its replacement by a new one—which now, after exilic editing, serve the overriding purpose of explaining the final disaster. The narrative of the disaster becomes, so to speak, the prelude to restoration, a grand theological link between condemnation and the hope of acquittal. We are in sight of another watershed which divides the event proper—recorded and enjoyed for its own sake—from the interpretation of the event. Yet even on the downward road, when the idea seems to matter more than the actual event, the Hebrew passion for looking at the real world never quite capitulates. Even the Chronicler will still tell a story after the Exile.

10 *Beyond time*

Didactic narrative has a petrifying effect. It thrives on the repetition of slogans and it leads to a static faith. In Israel, however, the catastrophes of defeat and exile brought a new direction to the ancient art. Gone were the days when the recital of past liberations and conquests could adorn the festive day. From now on they require a new dimension. Events of history are not enough. The new perspective requires a narrative which can transform the future, gain a universal appeal, and look even beyond the end into cosmic realities.

We find this new perspective in the Priestly narrative and its acceptance of old myths in Genesis 1—11. The heirs of Ezekiel took hold of the old stories in the ancient Near East which had circulated there for many centuries. As we have seen Egypt and Mesopotamia had already set earthly events against a cosmic canvas. Homer had told the exploits of heroes who served the sport of the gods. The tragedians had refined the nature of the conflict, and the philosophers had abstracted their ideas from the myths. The Hebrews proceeded differently and developed neither tragedy nor philosophy. Instead they came to terms with the same problems of existence by their unique tradition of Creation and Fall. The way had already been paved before the Exile in the great narrative schools, such as the Yahwist, where themes like Adam, Serpent, Garden, Expulsion, and Flood were already heard and controlled by the central motif, namely, the sovereignty of the Lord. But as yet the floating themes lacked unity.

The Priestly composition is severe and orderly. It controls memories of mythology, such as the blood which cries out for vengeance (Gen. 4) and the divine beings who mingle with women and produce giants (Gen. 6). The form of the myth persists in a curiously shortened form. In Genesis 1, for example, a liturgical rhythm dominates the story, as if the words were still part of a ritual, but the brevity of the account stresses the difference from ancient forms. Since there are no more gods, who intrigue, fight, copulate, procreate, eat and drink, laugh and cry, suffer and die, the narrator can afford to be brief. Israelite faith has transformed the tradition of the myths.

The narrative, then, unfolds a cosmic beginning outside history. This beginning before the beginning is the ultimate Word before all other words, the self-disclosure of God in his sovereign 'Let there be!' After this transcendent disclosure the narrator presses ancient themes into service. Adam, like the rebel Prometheus falls from on high; like Enkidu he loses his innocence; like Gilgamesh he must die and be outwitted by the serpent. But the same Adam is not only clay but also a living soul, is not confronted by bitter fate but by the Lord God who questions him: 'Where are you?' Similarly Cain, the murderous son and brother, is charged with the question: 'Where is your brother?' The transformation of the myth reaches its perfection in the Noah narrative, which retains the themes of the flood, the ark, the dove, in order to prefigure the future of man within the promises of the covenanting God. The form of the narrative no longer serves the boasting of Utna-pishtim, survivor of the waters, but the faith in a God who will save mankind at the end.

Nowhere do we find a closer integration of form and content than in the Genesis prelude. This narrative is so designed that it tells a timeless story in time. It has a beginning and an end, but it speaks of a God and a reality beyond both. Events happen 'in a place', but their world lies outside space. This form of narrative and faith converts the fantasies of the mythological age, for it reduces them all to one theological affirmation: 'In the beginning God created...'. All traditions originate from the Alpha point and converge upon the Omega point when the fulness of the creation shall be attained. Not only Abraham, Moses, David, and the prophets, are milestones on this road towards fulfilment, but the whole human destiny moves towards God. When the fourth Gospel resumes the cosmic 'In the Beginning was the Word' as the prelude to the narrative the reader is alerted to the final disclosure of Alpha-and-Omega in the face of the Man Jesus Christ. The narrative alone can unite the two natures, of God and Man. But in serving this theological purpose it is questionable whether it can really survive as a narrative. Soon it will be overtaken by abstract dogmatism. Only the rarest genius can speak of the Word-made-Flesh, of an abstract principle outside time and space, living in and as a person of flesh and blood, as an individual in a historical society.

The Priestly narrative makes the greatest demands on man's understanding, since temporal phenomena and eternal being are related to each other in both contradiction and complementation. Genesis 1—11 may not come into conflict with science, since these stories are not meant to be taken as science, but they cannot help arousing metaphysical speculation. The faith which believes in order to understand responds to this Word.

11 *Diary of the times*

After the Exile and the restoration of Jerusalem we get only glimpses of events and no continuous history. Just at a time when Greek historiography developed and parted company with the anecdotal style of such an entertaining geographer as Herodotus, when sombre Thucydides described political and military details, and Xenophon urbanely turned his own life story into an official account, the Hebrew scribes fail us. This seems particularly regrettable in view of the pre-exilic tradition of distilling history from a sequence of events. It may well be that the weight of salvation-history and theological framework crushed such attempts as were made and prevented their transmission.

Only a few bursts of somewhat parochial concerns come down to us through Haggai and Zechariah prior to the rebuilding of the Temple. Rebuke and exhortation bracket the story which is documented with dates and names. It is a simple record, appropriate for 'the day of little things', surrounded with rhetoric. The Chronicler attempts a more impressive programme in his outline of the rebuilding and fortification of Jerusalem. He also relies on dates, names, and documentation, such as Persian decrees, but unfortunately he is either too distant from the events, or his idealism causes him to stray into inaccurate chronology. In Ezra-Nehemiah things are said to have happened as they ought to have happened. Nevertheless the modern historian still finds ample treasure in the body of the work. The details compensate for the faulty chronology and doubts affecting the person and work of Ezra.

More significant, however, than the historical data of the Chronicler is the ideology behind the whole edifice of narrative. It patterns the past in the light of the present, and it moulds the present in the light of the past. The Chronicler stylizes history in order to legitimize, stabilize, and guide the post-exilic community. The situation during the Persian and Greek ascendancy demanded compromise, but not a compromise of identity. As so often happens in history, the razor's edge of principle could prove fatal unless support was given from both sides. The Chronicler tells the 'old story' to provide that support.

In this task he does not shirk dislocations of narrative. For example, the sequence of royal command, the implementation of the command, the climax of a religious celebration—as in Ezra-Nehemiah, a 'pair' which also suits his Moses-Aaron ideology—shapes the telling of the story. Yet he does not get stuck in artificial episodes, for the whole interpretation of history presses on towards a 'Jerusalem Rebuilt' finale. At the same time, the propaganda motif cannot drown the earthly and human aspect, especially centred in the person of Nehemiah, the ideal leader, builder, lawgiver, and reformer. The final chapter 13 is not absorbed by any pattern but stands in the text with a freedom which is as surprising as it is inexplicable. In chapters 5 and 6 we had already met the man in times of crisis, asking God to remember him for good and his enemies for their evil works. But at the end of his career we also seem to have reached a new turn of literary event.

Nehemiah's autobiographical account may be accepted as an authentic extract from something like a diary. He speaks not only as an eye-witness who has seen what goes on, but who has taken the lead in the community. He rebukes and exhorts while he identifies himself with the work at hand. He talks about 'them', the people, whether friendly, neutral, or hostile. He looks for, favours, and supports his allies, who soon appear as 'we' in the narrative. Their cause is also his, and God is 'our' God. Therefore Jerusalem rebuilding and rebuilt, repopulated and remanned, becomes again the nucleus of God in history.

But 'objective' history also serves as 'subjective' record. Nehemiah, not unlike the Greek historians, clears himself in advance against all possible accusations. As he asks to be 'remembered' by God he also deposits his protestation of innocence before posterity. This quasi-political flavour gives his Apology lasting value, for its form came to stay. Even if points of the story may sound trivial, the total impact of the Memorial ('Remember them—Remember me') can never be lost. Nehemiah creates a tradition of justification by works. Here is the beginning of that pragmatism which judges a man and his achievement by his success. Thus diary-entries and other records are geared into an area of evaluation. When centuries later a Josephus defends himself against charges of high treason and writes his *Jewish War*, which was to become a best-seller in Rome, he may have been influenced as much by Nehemiah as by Polybius or Julius Caesar. The deep-seated instinct to be found 'in the right', exonerated and vindicated, as well as to be perpetuated after death, accounts for this type of narrative and the faith with which it is handed on and read.

12 *Fiction*

It would be foolish to forget that however perfect the forms of narrative may have been, they could not have survived bar a participating interest among listeners and readers. The need to entertain was always there and should not be underrated. In the centuries succeeding the work of Nehemiah historical records seem to have counted for little, except among archivists, whereas the tale as such enjoyed increasing popularity. The folk-tale, traditional or invented, came into its own. It could provide, as, for example, in Job, an immediately engaging background. Here the story serves an enterprise on a vast scale. The prosaic beginning and end provide the stage for the poetic drama.

The short prologue in Job shows how a new dimension can be given to an old ill-luck story. The Satanic intervention transforms the simple original into a highly complex drama. The narrator, however, goes thus far and no further. When he appends a happy ending—the story of Job's restoration to good fortune—he rounds off the whole composition without any reference to the Satan. He has whetted our metaphysical appetite, and that apparently is enough for him and presumably also for us.

In this way the narrator succeeds not only in building the stage on which Job and his so-called friends can act out their endless speeches until the divine oracle can be heard. He also gets away from the kind of realism which would destroy his purpose. He eschews traditional names and Israelite history. He wants to portray God and Man in strictly unhistorical terms. Even if the themes of suffering and providence arise within Israelite concern he does not wish to place them there. He knows himself to be on stronger ground if he can go outside Jerusalem and Judah and Law. In this way, perhaps for the first time, the realism of fiction is deployed to obtain a more searing effect than actual events could ever furnish.

Prologue and epilogue must not be taken with a deadly seriousness which misses humour and irony. The author uses both for gaining spaciousness, just as Shakespeare, for example, uses the play within the play, or surrounds the play with an external dream-like plot. At the same time this device is not meant to lessen the import of the central plot. In Job, where the plot falls to pieces and nothing happens at all, the argumentation is in fact carried along by our knowledge of preceding events of which the speakers must be ignorant. In this way the narrator brings out his own faith that 'we' always move around blindly and never discern the whole truth. There are worlds within worlds, and we can only get at the truth through a perspective which we simply do not possess. The formal structure of Job suggests this perspective which lies beyond us.

The ancient stories with their antique diction provided this perspective. As Job recalled the world of the legendary sheikh of substance so Ruth also hails from the early days outside Israel. We are absorbed by her dignity in adversity, her loyal affection in the alien corn, a model of restraint and ultimate success. The legal tangle concerning property rights—first refusal, redemption, freedom to marry—hits us only indirectly, although it may have been the main problem in the original telling. As in the case of Job, the emphasis now lies on personal destiny and the place of virtue. Ruth, even more than Job, creates a new genre, for as we finish the little story we forget all about law, the place of foreigners in a closed society, the claims of the Davidic dynasty (as set out at the end), and simply accept it as a romance. Ruth becomes the exemplary tale of love and its conquest of all external hindrances. The form of the story guards against all mawkish abuses of sentiment and unnecessary embellishments. Its initial 'And it happened' sets limits of strict economy. The effect and depth of tension is obtained by the use of dialogue. Naomi, Ruth, Boaz go about their business, talk to one another, against a background of barley fields, reapers, threshing, sleeping, eating and drinking. But the form of the story makes not only for the concrete staging of life and love but also imposes upon the audience its own feeling and perspective.

The birth of the short novel and its growth is not easily traced, for the Bible has transmitted only very few examples. The little gem Jonah is a sailor's story. But far from building up a Hebrew Odysseus the narrator presents an anti-hero, the reluctant missionary, the Dove who represents Israel, in spite of himself. The sailors' panic in the storm, the large fish, the gourd, the Ninevites, and the animals, give an endearing quality to what might have become a dull missionary tract. Yet the shipwreck and rescue from the sea are not only in tune with popular taste in fiction but also recall traditional themes of salvation. Thus the story-teller combines comedy and seriousness with apparently effortless elegance. His anecdotal style accommodates a dialogue between God and Jonah in an almost naturalistic manner. He avoids farce by means of inserting a deeply felt prayer in the first half. In this way he balances the comedy with a formal solemnity.

The talent for the novel in pre-Christian Israel appears to have proliferated and is evidenced by the tales in the Apocrypha. Their exclusion from the Canon is, however, justified on formal grounds. The pious romance of Tobit is simply too long and lacks control. The author moralises on the propriety of burying the dead and then compensates for inadequate tension by substituting fantasy for invention. He flirts with magic and draws upon external improbabilities. On the other hand, the story of Susanna, which has been called the first detective story, is much too short to satisfy the reader. The heroine and her vilifiers are pale figures (as so often in this genre) and hardly more than names in a masque of chastity and lust. The reader is amused for a brief spell, and no more. The absence of characterization and psychological insight agrees with the simplistic construction of the tale.

The biblical novel or novelette appeals to the faith which

resides in the imagination. The reader or listener reacts to the behaviour of people whom he has never met in real life. He is not involved but sympathizes with the predicaments of Job, Ruth, and Jonah. The form of the story does not seek to bring about a passionate identification. It enshrines experiences common to all men everywhere. The man who suffers through no fault of his own, the girl who wins husband and children after widowhood, the coward who would evade his life's vocation on the sea of life, recognize themselves in the story. The novel offers the reader happiness and fulfilment in the area of sublimation, for he can appropriate for himself the happy ending which is the outstanding mark of the story.

Despite this considerable achievement in the realms of the imagination the novel as a form of faith did not expand and flourish. Pithy parables and religious allegories seem to have crowded it out both in Christian and in Jewish schools. Christians are even asked to repudiate fables, and it was left to pagan authors to make up stories to yield entertainment. The short biblical novel has never been reborn, for the modest plot could not contain the genius of the flowering culture of a later age. The subsequent creation of epics in prose, with external action and its impact on characters, quite surpassed the humble beginnings. The European novel, which has come to form the faith of the people quite independently, has perfected a tradition which is not interested in 'what happened, how it happened', but in the imagined human reaction to what inevitably happens all the time. Its links with the biblical tradition are, therefore, slender from a formal point of view.

13 *Propaganda*

Several reasons may be advanced for the failure of the Hebrew novel. The directness of the tenses, the lack of adjectives and adverbs, the stylistic rigidity of sentence structure, may well militate against the making of the kind of atmosphere without which a long novel cannot live. Development of character, density of plot, subtlety of relationships never approximate again the achievement of the Jacob-Joseph narrative, let alone surpass the Davidic nucleus. No such attempt appears to have been made. With the dawning of Roman power and strained social conditions in and outside Palestine the climate did not favour the cultivation of literary fiction.

The Maccabean resistance against Syrian rule and Hellenistic culture awakened a new interest in political and military writing. The writers wrote in Greek and used also sources, such as letters and eye-witness accounts, translated from Latin and Aramaic. The multilingual authors of 1 and 2 Maccabees employ Greek history writing for their own cause. The pietistic bias, especially of the latter, leads to exaggerations and even mistakes. Yet they rely upon chronological sequences, topological detail, military circumstance, personal bravura, to flesh out their new type of a secular history. The story is as long as the scroll allows. Thus the ancient heroic tale and the religious 'God with us' ideology reappear in a new guise. It feeds on and is also sustained by, its close link with festivals of all sorts which sprang up in the Hellenistic age, not infrequently in imitation of pagan holidays (e.g., Chanukkah = feast of dedication at the winter solstice).

The new patriotism also called forth a new model of historical fiction, of which the story of Esther alone found its way into the Old Testament. Written for the feast of Purim it celebrates the triumph of the queen and Mordecai, and thus of all potential martyrs. The bard summons the style of the old heroic past to give shape to the propaganda of the times. But national anxiety must often be content with formless products. The Rest of the book of Esther, of Judith, Bel and the Dragon —which among a stream of such literature happen to survive in the Apocrypha—underline the decadence of narrative. These stories about vindicated bravery suffer not only from religious naivety and even apparent godlessness, but a tedious imitation of the old style. The characterization of friends and foes operates with clichés; the action is predictable, the speech stilted. Judith's 'God with us' (11.11), for example, after the murder of Holofernes, cannot be taken seriously either as a tale told for children or as a morality paradigm for adults. The prototype of Jael in Judges 5 condemns this pastiche.

Nevertheless these stories must have proved their worth on the level of maintaining the faith. They probably served not only on the field of battle but also in the new ghettos in which the Jews confronted their Gentile neighbours. They are the stuff of which hagiography comes to be made. Perhaps we underrate their inherent worth, seeing that many centuries later, in totally different surroundings, the greatest European painters eternalized the ephemeral conflicts of Esther and Judith. They at least bestowed form and colour on a picture which the words had only poorly conveyed, but strongly suggested.

14 *Apocalyptic*

During the second century B.C. the Jews had to fight for their existence and identity as a people. This crisis never ended. War and national resistance evoked apocalyptic movements, and apocalyptic is the enemy of sustained narrative. The continuous flow of events, which peoples the stage with concrete persons, is arrested by the summons to battle. Persons are only codes. Obscurities and secret numbers oust the carefully observed behaviour of real men and women. The narrative, as we have known it in Israel, vanishes and is replaced by sectarian fantasy and uncontrolled utopia. The Apocalypses, handed down to us, for example, in the pseudepigraphical Writings are formless and bizarre oddities.

Yet there is at least one exception to this mushrooming decadence. The book of Daniel is certainly formless and not without bizarre touches, but it still tells stories in order to instil courage and fidelity. Taken by themselves the stories are terse in form and direct in tone. They do not pretend to take an interest in the character of the heroes or of the enemies. Only Nebuchadnezzar—even the name is wrongly spelt!—has some appeal, because he at least is not wholly good or wholly bad. But even he pales under the weight of the story, for his vision is but a means to work up towards a miracle and the inevitable happy ending. Belshazzar no more than outrages the audience in a predetermined melodrama. The reporting and the disclosure of visions serve as vehicles of, and for, the propaganda of the faith. Yet somehow the pathos of this bilingual book (Hebrew and Aramaic) somehow still grips the reader. Chapter 7, for example, celebrates the cosmic warfare between the beastly kingdoms and the humane rule of the Son of Man, the Saints, and the Ancient of Days, with such majestic symbolism that the reader or listener accepts unquestioningly the terms of the story.

The persistence of the narrative style in apocalyptic proves the surprising strength of the story form. Even after Daniel the utopianism of a sinless world, of a great judgement and a righteous Judge, of world-wide peace and eternal life, finds a host of authors who refurbish the old stories with a new futurism. Sometimes this takes merely the form of commentary, as in Jubilees which follows the outline of Genesis. The story of Ahikar, too, shows how ancient folklore can be worked up with further adventures and educational parables. Occasionally there really seems to be an advance under some original school of writers, who combine fantasy with a talent for descriptive narrative. Unhappily, however, it never gets very far. In Enoch chs. 17—36, for example, the hero journeys through the earth and the underworld, but his activity is restricted to his movement: he comes and he sees, but he does not do anything. Such passivity imposes severe limitations on the story. The episodes are too discontinuous to enlarge the basic form. There is no beginning, no plot, no counterplot, no real clash of interests. The tension is too artificial to warrant a dénouement. The jumpiness of style and monotonous use of stereotypes, cryptograms and secret numbers, finally dispels any belief in the story.

In short, the apocalyptic or utopian faith could not compromise with the tradition of narrative. As we have seen, the latter expresses an implicit belief in human freedom and in a meaningful relationship between God, the world, and men. In the apocalyptic vision all events are frozen, the trumpet sounds, and the books are open for the final tribunal. The story ends with the end of the story. It could not be otherwise.

15 *The story of stories*

The Christian narrative concerns Jesus of Nazareth, a Jew, who after a short life in public, was crucified in Jerusalem, in, or shortly after, A.D. 29. Reports about him derived from faith in him. A new epoch was felt to have dawned. His disciples proclaimed that he had been raised by God from the dead. They told a story which was already a tradition. Four of them composed formal Gospels, and one of them a work dealing with the Acts of the Apostles. The Church acclaimed these works as normative of their faith, thereby joining the new with the old. Whereas the Jews repudiated this claim of the new, and many Gentiles that of the old, the Christians insisted that the New fulfilled the old. Form and substance of the new narrative testified to its unity with the old faith in God. Yet the new wine burst the old wine skins, and the Christian narrative proves that mere continuity was not the aim.

The authors had to tell their story in strange circumstances. They spoke of events which for the most part had happened in a Hebrew-, or Aramaic-speaking context. Jesus probably had not uttered a word in Greek,[1] but the story had now to be told in the common Greek of the first century A.D. The authors and readers, however, also lived in a world where Roman law and administration functioned in Latin. If the author of Daniel moved in a bilingual world the evangelists had to be at home in three or four languages, thought-forms, and style. They had to tell a story and not to translate a document. They also must tell it in such a way as would interest, help, and further the Christian cause. But the story is not only for one community in one place, but also for posterity everywhere.

[1] There may have been a sort of 'Jews' Greek' which most Jews knew and spoke, not unlike the Yiddish of a later age.

In these circumstances the persistence of the ancient Hebrew forms comes as a surprise. One would have expected that at least one evangelist would turn the story of Jesus into a Greek tragedy, or that he would present his material as a Platonic dialogue or ethical dissertation. There is no trace of such an influence, nor indeed of any purely poetical cast of the material, whether in Greek or Latin. Similarly we are struck by the absence of certain Hebrew-Aramaic forms. The Gospels spurn the mechanics of apocalyptic coding, fictitious fantasy, or psalm pastiche, as we know them from Qumran. They contain no plain rite, liturgy, manual of discipline, admission of members and tests. If these areas of concern are touched at all, then they are thoroughly digested and brought within the umbrella of the narrative.

This narrative is clearly centred on Jesus. There are stories about him, introduced by formulae such as 'in those days', or 'after many days', 'at that time', 'then'. These stories work with the slightest touches of scene painting and reproduce speech, in monologue or dialogue, with marked economy, and distinct from the elaborate sermons. As in the Old Testament long speeches are only loosely attached to the story. Jesus dominates the narrative not only in speech but also in action. The concrete impression of his person is obtained by depicting his clash with hostile forces and his saving help in famine, sickness, and death. In the foreground Jesus appears as the prophet, simply because the narrative is cast in the prophetic mould.

Yet the narrative bursts this mould, for it is not the story of another Moses, Elijah, or Jeremiah. The narrator does not achieve his end by exaggeration. He could have heightened the tone by the use of the heroic style and by piling up fantastic similes or images. Instead he almost deliberately neglects this possibility. His comparisons—'like a dove', 'white as bleached cloth'—are few, and even in the Acts—'fiery tongues', 'angel's face', 'like scales'—he economizes. Instead the centre of the narrative is Jesus in his extraordinary 'ordinariness' which culminates in the Passion narrative. This story of the arrest, trials, and death of Jesus is the heart of something new, the final Gospel, a form of story shaped by the faith in the risen Christ.

The reconstruction of this nucleus, which is prior to all subsequent collections of the life and teaching of Jesus, hardly concerns us here. To this day the trial of Jesus remains the most controversial issue among scholars versed in Jewish law and Roman practice. Suffice it to say that historians and lawyers tend to accept the verisimilitude of the data which theologians rather coyly reject. For us, however, the point of interest lies in the Church's adherence to, and broadcasting of, a story which is, at least on the surface, depressing and by its very form opposed to the attitude of mind which we have called, somewhat baldly, faith.

It does not help us to argue that the sad story of man's misery and dying goes back several millennia. It is, of course, true that, as we have seen, the melancholy fate of Gilgamesh is echoed in many biblical stories, but the trial and death of Jesus cannot be compared with it or the end of Samson. Nor is Saul's suicide a parallel which throws any light upon our problem. The fact is that the whole Passion narrative stands in stark contrast to Hebrew and non-Hebraic accounts of heroic deaths or martyrdom. Consequently it does not evoke the kind of response on our part which the death of Socrates or Judas Maccabaeus or other great men may release. This feeling of mournful admiration or elated gratitude becomes the heroes' passing, but has nothing to do with the Passion narrative. Significantly, the former accords with heroic music, as in funeral marches; the latter cannot be rendered in this manner at all. Both hero-worship and pity are equally excluded by the story.

What, then, are the reactions which the original story desires to cause? Clearly, it is not a comforting story which makes dying more palatable. Even if read in the light of the sequence —belief in the Resurrection—the story is dark. This darkness does not deserve, or aspire, to be called tragic. The inevitability of the death of Jesus may appear to spell out tragedy, but the tone of the story does not. There is too much factual murder in its substance. The outline is strictly chronological and the narrator moves from place to place. The ordinariness of the event governs the low key of the narrative. Even the few tokens of decency which are reported—such as the women's relative courage—serve only to enhance the general sordidness of physical humiliation. The style of the narrative gives us no freedom to breathe; there is no distance between reporter and auditor. This directness rules out literary finesse, and remarkably the Church's transmission of the story has, with a few exceptions (Pilate's wife) resisted the temptation of adorning the account. The answer to our question is not difficult: the primary purpose of the memorial is to arouse fear and indignation. If these things happen in the green tree, what is to be expected at the end of the age? If the people of the Law and Roman justice perpetrate this sort of crime, what hope remains for mankind? Despair of the human situation, paradoxically, reiterates the 'things that happened'. Crucifixion lies over the whole world because of its sin. The Passion narrative enshrines a total repudiation of the human status quo. It sees death as the final answer to guilt. Jesus betrayed, arrested, denied, tormented, accused, sentenced, executed, forsaken, becomes, through the narrative, the norm of our malign destiny.

Yet the same narrative, far from buttressing belief in a total absurdity, asserts the exact opposite, a norm of providential fulfilment. The victim Jesus is shown as the priest who gives his life freely and in accordance with all the expectations of the Messianic hope. The redemptive pattern not only reconciles us to the murder, but turns the nihilistic events into disclosures of unprecedented Grace. The narrator weaves all the threads of horror into his canvas of fulfilment, so that the items of humiliation are seen to belong to that of exaltation too. Passover and Atonement rites and beliefs more than illumine the death of Jesus: they give the Passion narrative its general shape and its detailed and specific quality.

In the unadorned Passion narrative, as in Mark, this link with the universal past is far from obvious. If it were not for the Passover date and milieu one might miss it altogether, and if it were not for Paul one might well wonder whether, in fact, the early Church told the story with reference to the redemption from Egypt, freeing from slavery, and a new Moses who expiates for his brothers and intercedes for them. Paul had thus connected the story of 'How Christ suffered' with a 'Why and Wherefore?' in which he relied not only on a knowledge of Isaiah (esp. 52—53) but also a living and existentialist identification of his hearers with the portrayal of the Servant. But Paul had not invented this decisive interpretation. He had never received the reportage of the death of Jesus apart from its meaning, namely, that 'he died for our sins'. This meaning had shaped the facts a long time before the Gospels were written.

The Passion narrative is, therefore, inseparable from a long and complex story which is not told, but assumed. But even more bewildering and crucial is its connection with the Resurrection. It is certainly not a vulgar success or fairy story, in which the dead is suddenly found alive—whether through enchantment or some trickery. Recent attempts to foist such a cheap dénouement on the mystery have failed. Nothing could be more alien to the tradition than a Passover plot, with Jesus either pretending to have died, or pretending to be alive, with the body playing a sort of evidential piece to defeat the authorities.

The Resurrection, as Paul already states in his summary of received truths (1 Cor. 15), stands at the further end of the narrative, but is not part of it. True, there are a few resurrection stories, though Mark has none and ends significantly on the note of fear. But, in any case, they only matter in as far as they testify to the faith in the risen Christ, which has already interpreted the death of Christ as an accepted sacrifice for the beginning of the new life. In this way the future illumines past Passovers and present suffering as focussed in the death of Christ.

The four Gospels are the first normative redactions of this faith. They prove that much freedom remained to shape the material within the given tradition by going behind the death of Jesus to delineate his life. The conviction that 'Christ our Passover is sacrificed' and that 'God has raised Jesus' did not quench the desire to tell, write, and receive further accounts of the Man who died under Pontius Pilate.

16 *John's Paradox*

The problem now to be faced concerns the story of Christ in its four versions. Can it really be called a narrative at all? Or should it frankly be classed as a proclamation or preaching, surrounded with anecdotal material? The last of the Gospels, namely John, which surprisingly became popular only in the second century, shows the problem in its acutest form. Some would disqualify John as a story-teller, whilst others turn to him as the supreme narrator. Such a discrepancy of opinion must be due to more than the subjectivity of feeling among readers and critics.

The fourth Evangelist certainly reduces action to a minimum, for it only serves to underpin speech and controversy. His descriptive powers seem negligible, although it must be admitted that he somehow contrives to create atmosphere. Jesus at Cana, or at the well, or outside the tomb of Lazarus, is imprinted on the memory of most readers even after a first impression. Characterization is shadowy, and this is particularly strange, seeing that the subject of love is a constant theme in John's polyphony. But the usual forms and expressions of love, of lovers and beloved, are tacitly dismissed, for John not only eschews human passion in his composition, but also excludes the common dramatic heritage of the ancient world. He could have enlisted Chronos and Zeus, Agamemnon and Orestes, on the one hand, and Abraham and Isaac, Saul and Jonathan, David and Absalom, on the other, to render his portrayal of Father and Son more tangible and appealing than it is. But his Father and Son are 'not of this world', and the figures from the past do not interest him.

John's disclosure is given us solely through the truth of the Word, and the stories mirror the truth. He bends independent Christian traditions to his one over-riding purpose of verbalizing God's revelation in Jesus. The narrative, therefore, is not meant to stand outside the orbit of faith, for the story is the faith or it is nothing at all. He works over such sources as circulated in the churches and brings them together in a succession of stages. In his final rendering Jesus is known to the believer in the same story in which he is, ironically, exposed to misunderstanding on the part of the unbeliever. John stresses the double meaning of the story which polarizes the hearers. It is a testimony against the 'Jews', not in an anti-Semitic and racial context, but in a strictly religious, perhaps even local and denominational, sense. His narrative is always polemical and even takes care of the Baptist and his followers. He openly regards it as a weapon against lies and darkness and for truth and light.

Given this close relationship between faith and story the reporting of events must take second place. Yet John does tell a story and is not content to argue as in a Platonic dialogue or to play the part of the accuser as in ancient Hebrew disputes. The story material means more to him than mere evidence in a case of law. Occasionally the story even takes command—as in the Feeding of the Five Thousand, which, like the Passion narrative, he shares with the other Evangelists.

The story, then, is important because it is a means to an end. It is told to strengthen belief in Jesus as Son of God and to encourage the believer. The signs and wonders of Jesus are not only told so that similar works may be achieved, but also that they may disclose something else, i.e., the pre-existent Glory, which the Christ had with the Father. Thus the narrative points to reality beyond the earthly events, and especially in Part I (1.19—12.50) the Book of Signs works towards a climax of the knowledge of the Transcendent through an observation of temporal and spatial sequences. But these sequences are not symbolical as ideas, without flesh and blood; on the contrary, the God-in-Man walks, eats, works, and suffers in the flesh. He is not a god among mortals, nor mere man, nor a cypher of an indistinct transparency for the incomprehensible divine substance. He is the wedding guest, the stranger by the well, the healer, the master of bread and water, and he takes shape before our eyes as no symbol ever could. The presentation is such that he is central to all peripheral events and people. Yet whether he is really known, or meant to be known as he really is, cannot be answered. The Johannine Christ is the man unlike all other men and yet no man is after this story felt to be human apart from him. He is the norm: *Ecce Homo!*

The appeal of the Johannine Christ to our innate sensibility has varied over the centuries. Whether great or little, there can be no doubt that the Fourth Gospel may well be the decisive cause for the demise of the Christian narrative. There could be no other Gospel after its inclusion in the Canon, for it spelt out a finality of its own. Even imitations of the form could not succeed. Instead it evoked something quite new, namely, the portrayal of Jesus the Christ. The story led to iconography.

Despite the prohibition of images and much reserve Christian imagery slowly took root in the soil of the Fourth Gospel. Whether the face of Jesus was ever visualized as 'Semitic' remains uncertain. In the fourth century the beardless Christ, dressed in a toga, is already Hellenistic, Apollonian, youthful, and beautiful. Yet the Johannine deposit can also be recognized, first in the Shepherd surrounded by his sheep, and then, in the East, in the dark-haired and bearded prophet, who soon confronts the beholder in judgement, the Byzantine Pantokrator, whose glance abstracts the subject from the trivialities of earthly events. The narrative has become enshrined in mystical contemplation.

We cannot here pursue the strange sea-change which the Fourth Gospel was still to suffer in later centuries. The human response always seems to have remained alive. The implicit austerity of the narrative agreed with the experiences of communities and individuals. But during the Renaissance a change occurred, first in Italy, and then in the rest of Europe. The Christ portrayed by the great masters, such as Leonardo, Raphael, Donatello, is still 'Johannine', but the departure from tradition gathers pace. European masters of the sixteenth and seventeenth centuries have converted the transcendent Shepherd and Lord into a brother of men. Inexplicably an almost feminine admixture to the original portrayal leads to a grave distortion, and we are not very far from the 'Good Shepherds' of sentimental piety and worthless clichés.

This development of a counterfeit Christ points to the problem inherent in the narrative of the Fourth Gospel. How could the story ever authenticate such an absurd interpretation? This deviation from the truth was by no means confined to pictures, but may be found in the whole pietistic-sentimental exegesis of the Fourth Gospel. Indeed, the popularity of the story until recently was largely grounded in the agreed misrepresentation. Yet when we return to the text we fail to find any obvious reason for this abuse.

Now the pendulum has swung to the other extreme and the Johannine Christ is seen much more in line with modern portrayals of Christ, which are abstract and descriptive of alienation and torment. The narrative, too, is understood as a searing indictment of humanism and humanistic religion. It pairs down, as from the beginning, the accumulation of false Christs to the One Word which was made flesh. It remains the story which explodes the eternal in this hour. The divine glory (Gk. *Doxa*) stands here for ever as the human paradox.

17 Mark's Secret

The three synoptic Gospels also culminate, like John, with the Passion story, but in every other respect they shape their Gospel differently. Mark's is the first orderly account, which may go back to Peter in Rome. Mark integrates mission preaching and memorabilia of Jesus in order to compose a progress report. That at least is the outward form. But behind the outline of events lies a complex history, which to the reader is no longer obvious, until he makes himself remember that Mark's 'events' happened at least four decades earlier than their publication in Gospel form. Moreover, they happened in an Aramaic-speaking setting; now they are presented in Greek to a church which exists in a Roman world.

The author is not merely a redactor of tradition. His is an ideological stance which compels him to find a form for which there is no precedent. He sets himself to proclaim the Kingdom of God on behalf of the Son of Man. This Son of Man is the Christ whom God has sent into the world, the new David whose claims to absolute sovereignty must be unfolded before the world rushes to its ruin.

The models of secular writing may be known to Mark, but he eschews their use. He is not another Josephus, nor indeed another Julius Caesar. Even the style and arrangement of the books of the Maccabees do not suit him. If he is acquainted with Qumran-Essene or Rabbinical works, such as commentaries, he shows no interest in them. He does not seem to know Palestine at all well and the emerging Judaism he dislikes strongly. Yet he is sufficiently Jewish not only to locate his story in Galilee but also to be influenced by Jewish forms, customs, and traditions, such as no Gentile Christian could ever have been attached to. He comes nearest the history writers of the Old Testament, both in feeling and in style. Like the compilers of Samuel and

Kings he combines a concrete, eye-witness, on-the-spot technique[1] with a wider perspective, which gives the spectator both precision and roominess of vision. We seem again to be following the fortunes of David by means of a lively participation and almost naïve directness of narrative. Yet this part of the storytelling is balanced by the conviction that the new Exodus has been, and is being, offered to the people of God. Hence the Moses-Exodus motif also affects the author's presentation. He is not only narrator, but also enthusiast, engaged with eschatological fervour.

This enthusiasm controls the data—geographical, numerical, and even liturgical—at Mark's disposal. He works up to certain peaks in the narrative, such as the miracles, the Transfiguration, the Finale of Passover and Passion, and the enigmatic ending which promises an appearance in Galilee. But the enthusiasm does not kill the ordinary world. This integration of disparate materials is crowned by the inclusion of stories within the story, namely, the so-called parables.

These typically Jewish *meshalim* present an enormous difficulty to the present reader, but they must have been even more refractory to Mark at the time of writing. These similes taken from life, whether extremely brief or somewhat extended, do not immediately interlock with the reality of Mark's concern. There is little doubt that Jesus had told such stories and that some circles had preserved them. In his mouth they had been 'language events', suitable for, and provoked by, special circumstances. Homes, fields, markets, courts, etc. had always elicited anecdotes with a special point. For centuries polemics had flourished on all sorts of topics by the provocative use of the story. Jesus was acting both as prophet and teacher when he talks of sowers sowing seed (ch. 4).

But this connection was lost when the Evangelist selected this

---

[1] Cf. Mk. 5.21–43 for the achievement of dramatic tension: Jesus on the way to Jairus' house is intercepted by the woman with the issue of blood. Luke retains the order (8.40–56), but Matthew loses the effect through drastic cutting (9.18–26).

relatively small material from the much larger deposit called 'parables'. The audience had changed as much as the point of the telling. Mark subordinates the story-in-the-story to his single perspective which is that of the Kingdom of the new David under God. The end-stress or, in modern jargon, the warhead which explodes is directed against those who resist the power of the Word. The secret of the Messiah, wrapped up in parables, remains undisclosed to them like a dark riddle. In this way Mark has transposed the key of the original.

Does the total form of Mark, then, betray a case of fraudulent conversion? A long line of critics—from Reimarus to Wrede and thence to Eisler and Brandon—have regarded this Gospel as a political document. Even if they would not call it a manifesto they equate it with propaganda pure and simple. But propaganda for what? As we have seen, the narrative almost always overlaps with some kind of propaganda. If we, for example, refer to the Davidic element in Mark we concede a propagandistic strain, for as soon as Jesus is portrayed in some fashion as a new David he cannot be anything else but a political figure. The question, therefore, is more precisely what political figure lies behind Mark and what Mark has made of Jesus through his telling of the story in the way he did.

There are many variations on this theme. For example, to follow a broad outline, Jesus of Nazareth is alleged to have been a political firebrand, anti-Roman, anti-Jewish-establishment, and possibly even a violent guerilla fighter. He was captured and killed, and his followers remembered him and formed traditions about him. Mark, so goes the case against him, turns this Jesus into his exact opposite, a non-violent and pro-Roman collaborator. Mark seeks a *modus vivendi* for a Gentile Christian Church within the limitations of Nero's Rome. He must impute the guilt to the Jews in order to ingratiate himself and his community with the authorities. He furthers the Christians' cause by using the memories of a Jewish Messianic sect, which originated in the thirties, to support the Roman Church in the sixties. Thus he turns the cult of the patriotic deeds of a Jewish martyr into that of an anti-Jewish saviour.

Apart from the inherent improbability of this trickery and its success, of a scheme of lies to be good news in any moral sense, it is hard to account for the survival of the Galilaean milieu and the whole Jewish connection. The substance of the story seems quaintly out of place in this world of assumed propaganda. Once again it is the total form which demands our attention.

But what is this form? It is far from self-evident and has evoked too many theories to be enumerated here. But when all is said and done, here is a dramatic story without introductory beginning and, as it now stands, without a satisfactory end. Its inner coherence does not derive from proclamation, despite kerygmatic words, but rather from the visualization. Mark uses traditions by which he 'sees' Jesus in Galilee, dealing authoritatively with demons, the sick, and nature. But Jesus is also human and weak, and Peter is even weaker, a little man among little people without any antique heroism. Consequently for Mark events and people matter, and he brings the utmost seriousness to the concerns of fisherman, tax gatherers, and the poor. In this almost provincial way, with government and police in the background, he addresses the world of men and women and children, offering them escape from slavery. His story is the 'seen' liberation from oppression, but the freedom which he offers is not achieved by violence, but by the identification with Jesus in his suffering. Though Pauline in this essential, Mark sticks to his progressive story, for he sees Jesus very much 'after the flesh'. He does not play with Pauline agnosticism about the earthly Jesus, nor with Johannine 'panels' or signs. The story of Jesus the Christ is the norm of belief, and Markan faith articulates the whole of experience, to the point of suffering and death, as Good News, evangel. His story is devised as a bridge between what has happened and what will happen: from Galilee to Galilee, from misery to felicity.

18 *Promise and fulfilment*

Matthew and Luke probably knew and used Mark. Like the latter they fall outside the literary forms of their day, for being 'Gospels' they use narrative in a specific way of faith. In this usage they differ markedly. For example, Matthew and Luke give an account (non-Markan) of the healing of Centurion's servant (Matt. 8; Luke 7). Both gospels put this event after giving the great sermon of Jesus. For Matthew the healing discloses the power of God irrespective of distance and physical touch. His context is still the fight for the universality of the Christian message against the resistance still offered in certain quarters. Luke, without denying this aspect, is more interested in the centurion's merit and humility. He puts into his mouth almost liturgical language—'Lord, I am not worthy ...'—and stresses his actively trusting faith. Luke's centurion appears again in Cornelius in the very long narrative now found in Acts 10. These different nuances of stress help us to place the Gospels in their respective milieu of life and concern.

The Matthaean form of the Gospel conspicuously unites contrasting and even contradictory features. On the one hand the Gospel stands for law and rigorism, and has even been called a witness against Pauline teaching; on the other, it passionately accuses the Pharisees of a harsh and hypocritical legalism. Again, Matthew preaches a Way and sets it forth like a manual of behaviour in the Christian community; yet some of his material is wholly different in character and almost legendary, like the coin in the fish's mouth or the intervention of Pilate's wife. This paradoxical trait seems deep-rooted, for the Gospel is both aggressive and even abusive as well as apologetic and defensive.

This paradoxical tone is not only on the surface. The author preaches 'fulfilment' as his leading motif, but he stands aloof from tradition. Similarly he composes his Gospel like a liturgist, yet he tells the story with unique concentration and successfully. Though ecclesiastical in tone it is anticlerical in its polemic (e.g., ch. 6). Matthew writes as and for the individual Christian in a setting that is altogether communal. He is not far from the organization and problems of the Qumran community, but the over-arching belief in the Resurrection of Jesus makes for an abrupt parting with all Jewish sects. Nevertheless, he is still sufficiently in touch with them to give his answer to their anti-Christian stand. The Lord's Prayer, for example, may be read as his reply to the Jewish Eighteen Blessings (*Shemoneh Esreh*) and an answer to the Council of Jamnia of A.D. 90. He operates, as do his opponents, with *logia* or proof-texts which, however far-fetched at times (e.g. Jesus the *Nazaraios*, 2.23), link the revolutionary present with the past.

His use of the Parable, too, illustrates his originality. For him the Parable is not a story, *tout court*, nor a fable or allegory. As in chapter 13 he uses the parable almost as a quasi-legal device, applicable to 'cases'. The selected audience knows of the case and the parable evokes the comment, as it should. Matthew shows himself as a master of combining law and story (*Halakah* and *Haggadah*) as well as of teaching and proclamation (*Didache* and *Kerygma*). He combines a vast range of formulae, quotations, legal definitions with areas of salvation and judgement, and the narrative is the thread which provides continuity.

If it were not for the strength of the narrative Matthew might be explained as a handbook for teachers and leaders in the community. But it was obviously more than that from the start. It reminds one most of Isaiah, from whom the author quotes so often and so passionately that he may well have been trained at Qumran. Such a connection would also explain in part the apparent contradictions suggested above. Matthew is a Jew who no longer waits for the Messiah, because his Messiah has come and begun his world-wide reign. He belongs to a persecuted minority, which despite its troubles feels a sovereign power in its midst. He looks to the future for the vindication of faith in the risen Messiah, and he looks to his coming in the context of the end and the judgement of the present world.

The narrative which reflected these tensions became the 'royal' Gospel, because it succeeded in the realistic presentation of the sovereign Christ in a historical community which suffered in its mission. It brought a sense of triumph in deep darkness. This triumphalism, later distorted and even abused, derives from the final promise 'I am with you', which is the goal of the whole narrative. Matthew for the first time places the Galilean Jesus in the everywhere and always of all mankind. The baptism of the world is seen as the fulfilment of this Gospel.

19 *A new map*

The inner contradictions come to an even greater climax in Luke–Acts. In his two-volume work the author also combines *Halakah*, or ethical teaching, with *Haggadah*, appealing narrative. But whether this narrative is based upon reliable sources or any sources at all, whether it reflects events which happened, whether the author is Luke, Paul's friend (2 Tim. 4.11), a doctor and artist, who with amazing skill creates the effect of distance and enjoyable perspective for the reader, whether he follows classical models like Thucydides in the use of speeches, or rather his contemporary Josephus in sketching biographical details—all this, and more, must remain the subject of unresolved controversy. There is no agreement even as to whether Luke always understands his material and knows what he is saying. Some commentators depict him as a tailor who stitches together his material with little understanding, beyond the use of catchwords, whereas others regard him as a subtle theologian, even of the second century, who most skilfully, and irresponsibly, combats Paul and Paulinism by introducing into Acts a Paul who never existed at all.

Luke does not fare well when seen by some as a propagandist, a representative of early anti-Semitism, pro-Roman, who uses Christian belief to create and sustain an infant Catholicism. He is suspect of, even hated for, undermining the Pauline preaching of Galatians and Romans by giving us instead a Paul who is citizen of the world. His Gospel, then, is 'another' Gospel—authoritarian, Gentile, sacramental, optimistic, cultural—which defuses the eschatological tension and throws off the Jewish anchorage.

No doubt Lukan form goes hand in hand with Lukan faith, but his 'story' defends and validates claims which cut across such a radical repudiation of the author. The Church's expansion from Jerusalem to Rome is his theme, for in it he sees the providential pattern. The divine plan is as central to him as to Deuteronomy. God's foreknowledge governs events, not automatically, but to establish our freedom, for God is with us in the new Exodus for which Christ suffers to bring salvation to the world.

The divine plan can be gauged by vignettes in which God is seen to have acted. Thus Luke unfolds the strangest drama, beginning with the annunciation, the conception and birth of two babies, the mingling of angels and shepherds, a census. No one can accuse him here of dropping the Jewish, supernatural, eschatological form of presentation. We do not have to go to Greek authors nor to Josephus but merely to the book of Samuel to find our literary precedent. He continues with the basic Markan outline in the spirit of the Exodus tradition. Jesus teaches, heals, exorcises, forgives, prays, feeds, and blesses the people. He is the Messiah-Servant, poor, celibate, obedient, lovely as well as beloved, recalling features of the Davidic youth. Through the narrative the Servant becomes, almost imperceptibly, Kyrios, Lord. In him God confronts Israel with himself and continues to do so, for the murdered Jesus is not physically absent, but risen and present, even for Israel, through the Spirit among those who await the Kingdom. The disciples' acts are still continuous with the divine plan, and therefore everything works for good, as they gather and disperse, preach and work miracles, suffer and escape. The 'real' world, hostile and often absurd, mingles, as at the beginning, with the angelic and apocalyptic 'reality'. Jerusalem is and remains the centre of the risen Christ, for even Samaria, Antioch, Caesarea, Damascus, and the cities of Asia pledge their loyalty to the Apostolic origin.

When Luke 'sets everything in order' for Theophilus, and for all posterity, he is not carried away by the geographical sweep of the triumph of the Gospel. His book is not a traveller's tale or guide, though every place on Paul's route contributes to the whole. Climax follows climax, but the Spirit of God remains constant. Similarly Paul does not replace the centre of the narrative. Even when the narrator shares his company, and indicates his presence in the 'we' passages, his hero does not oust God. When Paul leads the crew to safety at the shipwreck and reaches Rome in an almost serene finale he also fits into the great design, just as he did earlier during his inexplicably surprising behaviour at Jerusalem.

Luke does not write theology any more than he records events. The tradition of Joseph and the Exodus, and of the early history of Israel in Canaan, forms his narrative. We may perhaps detect also a Homeric streak of heroism, a Virgilian aura of tender concern and adventurous courage, a Hellenistic mannerism, a Galilean bias in favour of the outcast, and possibly a personal friendship with Mary and 'the ladies', and an interest in medicine. These elements, as often denied as affirmed by modern scholars, never obfuscate the primacy of the narrative itself. Luke's genius bends tradition and current forms and fancies to his faith which transfigures Crucifixion, and with it the whole human condition, into a triumph of eternal love. He may rightly be called the first Christian artist for he casts the infinitely complex and disturbing into a beguiling story of the transformation of the world.

Luke, therefore, brings to a fine point the ancient belief that the narration of human affairs belongs itself to the spiralling faith which will conquer the world. He is not a symbolist who works with signs, nor is he indebted to the notion of the seamless robe, through which all things and people are somehow connected, as the islands with the main. These somewhat static categories cannot contain his dynamic and personal approach to reality. Jerusalem is for him not yet a heavenly or supernatural focus, but the constantly receding centre from which the church rises in a cone, advancing continually in faith and visible expansion. His religious optimism is deeply based upon Jesus crucified and risen and spills over into the history of all man, not in order to be diluted by a pan-Hellenistic 'religion'—which he ironically portrays in Paul's visit to Athens—but so that joy and blessing shall boldly and freely come to the whole world through the risen Christ. Luke's last words, in the Gospel and in Acts, declare, as always, the target for the spiralling faith-narrative: 'praising and blessing God; teaching the things pertaining to the Lord Jesus Christ with all courage and without hindrance'.

20 *Memorial and Testament*

All the four Gospels converge upon the Last Supper and the Crucifixion as the climax of the story. If further Gospels had been transmitted to us, or should be found in the future, the portrayal of these events would no doubt afford us even greater diversity than at present. But the surviving traditions, though few in number, describe the institution of the Last Supper with distinct perspectives of their own. The close relationship between faith and reportage reaches its summit at this point.

The Johannine narrative is perhaps the most surprising in that it does not openly include a report of the institution of the Last Supper. The Evangelist takes its existence, and also knowledge of its existence, for granted. He expatiates on the nature of the Living Bread and stresses the need of man to share in the only Bread which fills the hungry. The teaching has replaced the descriptive narrative, though the Feeding of the Five Thousand is notably retained by John as a kind of peg on which to hang the teaching. The eucharistic union having been thus established well before the Passion John is free to concentrate on the meaning of the rite. He associates the washing of the feet with the great commandment of Love. Throughout he hints at the event without actually describing it. The narrative thus comes through by suggestion rather than by words and recital. Yet this is only possible because there lies behind this mysterious silence the knowledge that Jesus used a fragment of Bread, in the accepted manner, to denote the ritual of the Coming One (the *Aphiqoman*, or crumb of *Pesach*, Passover).

The Johannine silence stands alone, but the other Gospels prove that the tradition was always terse, if not secret. It was never embellished but always retained the tone of extreme crisis. When one considers the amount of detail that went to the description of an ancient banquet one cannot help being struck by the omission of all facets of the meal. To this day, for example, we cannot tell whether a lamb was eaten or not. The paucity of information comes as an even greater shock when one considers the context of the narrative. The preparation in the Upper Room promises a great deal more, but after Jesus' denunciation of Judas there is a gap. This sudden change of key and surge of drama are the chief common characteristics of the tradition. Within that narrow confine the Evangelists bring out their own standpoint. Mark shows how Jesus unites the community in a sacrificial existence. According to him the bread-breaking fellowship shares not only a meal but anticipates the Kingdom of God. Matthew, however, while not denying this eschatological expectation, uses practically the same words to identify the rite with the Jewish Passover, the advent of the New Year, and the Atonement. Matthew integrates the institution with Jewish liturgy and moves within a hierarchic area, and not a layman's society, such as Mark's. Luke stands in his own tradition of faith and interprets the institution as a foretaste of freedom. Like the Deuteronomist, his model, he celebrates the liberation from bondage and anticipates the great feasting which redemption ushers in. The reversal of the order of bread and wine in his shorter version may well be due to Luke's reading of the institution as a celebration first and foremost. In placing the cup first, he is certainly much nearer the original *Kiddush* (= Blessing) said in any Jewish home before the proceedings proper.

The liturgical action and the story were united from the first, if Jesus kept (or anticipated) *Pesach* with them before his arrest. The traditional preparations in the house of a Jerusalem disciple are not described in detail, however, because the Jews would have taken them for granted and the Gentiles at a later date could not be interested. The later symbolism (the roasted shankbone; the hard egg; the bitter herb; the mixture of nuts, honey, and spice; the salt) had not yet been regulated, but the several cups (four, plus that of Elijah) may already have been customary. The usual element of family fun, however, is totally absent from the New Testament narrative. The story of the Pass-over, therefore, is strangely overtaken by the drama of the expected betrayal and arrest. Nevertheless, although Jesus may not have taken his share of the lamb, the order of the feast was observed: candles lit, blessings pronounced, hands washed, *matzah* broken—with one half kept, the bread of affliction which becomes the bread of the Coming One. The formula 'This is the bread' brings Jesus to the story (in answer to the question 'Why...?'), his own *Haggadah* of salvation. He probably paralleled the plagues of Egypt with the plagues of his own time, though time may have been too short, after Judas' depar-ture, to relax to savour the details of the past. Moreover, Jesus must press on to the new covenant, its substance and ratification. The story of the past led to the present, and both were set forth in the rite of thanksgiving (drinking of the second cup). Perhaps it was only at this point, when the covenant was made articulate, just before the meal, that Judas left. Jesus' *Haggadah* may have provided the needed impetus to break with him. The story-teller regards Judas' desertion as integral to the whole. His departure is the prelude to the sharing of the *Aphiqoman*, the bread of the Coming One.[1]

We know that the narrative of the institution of the Eucharist is earlier than the Gospels, but not whether it was a formula of consecration in the early church or at what point it was recited in such a liturgical manner. The passages in 1 Cor. 10 and 11 defy a straightforward thesis, though they are not in themselves obscure. The Apostle cites the tradition as something received by him as by all Christians, but in his context the 'memorial' simply acts as a moral challenge. He assumes that the story itself is a powerful accuser, that unscrupulous selfishness cannot be de-fended in the light of it, and that the very words will expose and penetrate the guilt of the community. The re-enactment of the Supper is primarily warning and judgement, and the emphatic commandment 'Do this!' links the narrative to the state of the recipients and matters such as eligibility and worthiness.

[1] from ἀφικνέομαι =I come (cf. Daube).

In subsequent centuries the place of the narrative in the faith of the Church still remained flexible, but the centre of its impact shifted to different areas, such as the distinction between inward and outward reality, the substance of Body and Blood, and the nature of the oblation. But even when a liturgical rigidity came over the tradition—first in Latin and then in modern tongues—the narrative was wont to reassert itself in the community. The very inclusion of the story in the rite, with the sequence of Blessing, Breaking, Giving, and Taking, made the formation of a static 'memorial', whether magical or pietistic, unacceptable.

The narrative always recalls the Church to an original covenant to which even the names given to the liturgy (Mass, Eucharist, Last Supper, Holy Communion etc.) are incidental and subservient. All the great reforms and struggles in Christendom converge upon the meaning of this innocently short report of Jesus' action and words during the night when he had been betrayed. They are the centre of controversy, but they are also the beacon which summons the faithful to unity and love.

This universal act of remembrance derives from the written and spoken narrative, recited at an altar or around a table, in community or to and by individuals, recalling the past and anticipating the future, releasing divine power and demanding homage, unfolding dimensions of suffering, tragedy, and sacrifice in a context of blessing and felicity. Thus the words signpost a wide and open road for all, made narrow by specific injunctions and set in well-defined areas, where man seeks God and God finds man. This journey, as inspired by the narrative, still continues to an unknown destination and remains the basis and test of what Christians call faith.

The modern narrative

PART II

The modern narrative

21 *The Christian Pattern*

Literary studies lack the approach and method of science. It is easy to propound theories, but it is impossible to verify them. We read stories and project a background into them which is often of our own making. Yet even if we tread unwarily on treacherous ground some advantage comes to us, if only certain theories come to look absurd. In the field of mythology, for example, the 'key to all mythologies' has never been discovered and we can be pretty certain that it does not exist. There are too many doors to be opened. We can read myths from all parts of the world and force upon them religious, or sociological, economic, political, or psychological structures, but our desire to obtain one general theory of myths will always be defeated by the multifarious and inconsistent richness of the material.

We have therefore good reason to abstain from a general theory of Christian narratives, even if the area is more compact and altogether controlled by the community's faith in Christ. But even in this small area totally different results are obtained dependent upon our ideas of what these communities were like. Thus form-critics are often not form-critics at all, looking at the form of the narrative; but rather they postulate the existence of a community which makes up and trades in reports which allegedly served the immediate practical needs. Unfortunately we work here with an enigma wrapped up in a puzzle. We tend to explain the narrative by the model of a reconstructed community, and we construct the community with the aid of the narrative. This method condemns itself by being subjective and arbitrary.

The pattern of the narrative can, of course, never be divorced from the writers and compilers who fulfilled the practical and liturgical needs of the community. But communities change, and sometimes their needs even more quickly. This is particularly true of New Testament times, when within the space of less than a century the scriptures spoke to and from churches which had very little in common with their founders, except the continuity of faith. But the scriptures had become unalterable and their pattern subsisted in a revolutionary situation. They proved the durability of the Word.

The Christian narrative thus came to make a claim to being the lasting and normative revelation. God is never directly present nor ever totally absent, and it is upon his unique Presence that the narrative converges. The scriptures are read to impart directly something of his hidden Presence. The delineation of events in a time process is not considered a hindrance but rather the fulcrum of the disclosure. There is a beginning and there is an end to the story, and in the middle there is change. Now the specific events which are reported and imply change (from hunger to satiety, from illness to health, from guilt to forgiveness) impart the Presence of God. He is apprehended through all levels of human experience, so that what was formerly unknown becomes known.

The Christian narrative blends corporate events and individual destinies. The reader and listener react also, mostly without being aware of the complexity, as members of the corporate body and as private citizens. Thus a vignette, such as Matthew's pearl in the fish's mouth, appeals to the Church in the pagan Empire and the individual Christian as a taxpayer. This story is only one of many which evoke a social as well as personal sense of obligation. The appeal is to the 'you' of the community, but the response must come from the 'Thou' of the members in that community. We enter a highly complex web of inter-relationships.

The tension between society and individuals belongs to the Christian pattern of experience. The story reflects the experience of Jesus. Like him the Christian lives in a hostile world whose laws he obeys. Hence life is not a quiet stream of birth, marriage, family, and death, but rather a dramatic conflict with forces superior to the members which make up the society. The Christian pattern of narrative reflects not only the conflict of Jesus, but also the paradox of all human beings who want peace and find war.

The story regards the outcome of the conflict as foreseen. The motif of the Son of Man 'must suffer' sounds in a melody which determines the life of all. But this determinism does not rule out freedom, for it deals not with puppets on a string but with humans who respond to whatever befalls them. The story reflects the further paradox that the whole universe hangs together within a grand design which offers freedom to those who accept it.

The result of actions and reactions is never wholly good or wholly bad, but a mixture of both. The Christian pattern is so conditioned by Crucifixion and Resurrection that a simple tale of prosperity or of meaningless ordeals cannot be told. Loss, and even catastrophe, are paired with gain and vindication. Everything appears to be for the worst and turns out to be for the best.

This Christian patterning of human experience bursts the terms of human self-understanding. The narrator projects the human conflict into something greater than itself. He operates with norms of correspondence. Nothing subsists in itself, everything is woven into a vast texture of relationships. The density of the story depends upon the texture, the togetherness of human beings in a demonic world. The events are not other-worldly, but they fit into a design which derives from, and leads to, another world.

This world is known to be invisible and intangible and is believed to be imperishable in contrast to the world which does perish. The concrete and temporal events which the story articulates are felt to be visitations from this eternal world. We belong to it though we have lost it. There may be meaningless events in time, or they may look meaningless to us, but the Christian perspective looks at them differently. They are to a varying degree knitted together into a purposeful process. Therefore man's life is a kind of pilgrimage from total loss to total gain. There are heroes on the way who typify the progress and fulfil the design. Abraham, Jacob, Joseph, Moses, and all the prophets and wise men are steps on the ladder to Jesus Christ. The chronological sequence is of little importance, for all becoming is hitched to the chain of Being. Not only is the Word made flesh, but the flesh of human endeavour—from the beginning to the end—is caught up and eternalized by the Word. Thus the 'simple' story turns out to be far from simple, for it relies upon the validity of the principle of correspondence.

This principle takes us to the heart of the feeling of antiquity. Mark's Gospel stresses it less than, say, the Epistle to the Hebrews, but it really pervades all Christian attempts of comprehending the Gospel. It can easily be abused in fantastic allegories, when almost anything can be made to correspond to anything. For example, lions and lambs can be made to stand for violence and non-violence, out of context and therefore unconvincingly. The story of the Good Samaritan or of the unjust Steward has had echoes in all ages of the most bizarre kind. The principle of correspondence, as we now see it, can become a weak spot of interpretation. Judas becomes everyone's enemy, Peter everyone's example. The path to eisegesis—reading anything into the story—is always open.

The Christian pattern evokes unconsciously the correspondence between the spatio-temporal event and the eternal meaning. The story does not prove, nor seeks to prove, this correspondence. It suggests the divine hand in the human fragmentation. It controls the formless and bizarre by the use of forms of realism. Thus the author of the Acts of the Apostles can report of Peter's liberation from prison in a matter of fact way, leaving the fantastic to the response of the perplexed community. He even mocks at those who misinterpret the events as visitations from the gods. An ironic sobriety gives the material an earthly directness. Yet the heavenly dimension is always implied.

The coherence of events and meaning gives solidity to arbitrary claims of correspondence. It helps the narrator to avoid allegorizing events and people. Thus, although Christ fulfils the Old Testament, he is not merely a replica of Moses, David, and the prophets. The contours of Christ are given in the portrayal of one Jesus, who recalls the type of lawgiver, king, and prophet, and yet retains the highest individuality. Later on these distinctions tend to become blurred, and just as it is said of Faustus that he sees Helen in every woman, commentators see Christ in every figure of the past. But story and faith are at their most vigorous when the distinctions coinhere in the whole without loss of individuality. These men and women act and suffer, talk and reply, in a unique fashion and thus fit into the eternal design.

The principle of coherence creates a problem of its own within the Christian pattern and this has proved obdurate to being solved throughout the centuries. It puts all other literary problems of the Bible in the shade. According to this principle all the stories ought to fit into an overall scheme, namely the Canon of Scripture. This term gives the illusion that a transcendental unity governs all the stories, and that, like an artificial yardstick, it can be applied everywhere. But the complexity of the material defies this kind of treatment. The stories do not 'make sense' because they all say the same thing. Different conceptions of God, of man, of the meaning of life, of morality, abound in them, since they come from and represent disparate epochs of history and geographical areas. Even the four Gospels, though they belong 'together', do not speak with one voice. The coherence is, therefore, the direct opposite of uniformity. As soon as a uniformity of faith is forced upon the narratives it distorts their genius. The extraordinary resilience of the Christian narrative rests upon a coherence which answers to the complexities of life.

The basic polarities of life and death, love and hatred, guilt and forgiveness, defeat and victory, war and peace, run through the whole Bible, and particularly the Gospels. Of all the writers Luke manifests the most striking and probably conscious, inclination towards a double focus in his composition. He portrays the divine disclosure with brush strokes of dark and light. The Lukan spectrum makes the reader feel that he need no longer register polarity as impossible or strange. It seems natural that angels and heavenly voices are tied in with shepherds and politics. The polarity converges upon the One, who as child and man is not less human because he is divine, nor less divine because he is human.

With Jesus as the centre of gravity the maximum tension between God and Man, Heaven and Earth, Eternity and Time, Infinity and Space, Perfection and Degradation, sustains the narrative. It cannot be broken down into any other order or system. If the picture were to lose its multi-dimensional form and its range of colour it would cease to be itself. Jesus is born into the Roman world and moves in the area of history, works as the Jewish carpenter in that of sociology (Galilean poverty and class structure), teaches as a Rabbi in that of ethics, and yields a complex character in that of psychology. But he is not remembered as an exponent of any of these, nor can he be comprehended by such studies. The coherent story is a Gospel picture and can be reduced to nothing else.

The narrative achieves this integration of polarities because that seems to have been the author's original purpose. The final unity is not a chance product, but a stylistic accomplishment. Many authors and redactors worked with multiple sources, some of which had a pronounced local flavour, but they did not stitch them together as they received them. Lists and memoranda could be contained in archives in an haphazard fashion, but the deeds, sufferings, and triumphs of men had to be commemorated differently. Luke worked in this tradition, bringing to a fine point the belief that one life depicted can disclose the meaning of all contradictions. He does not pioneer, but perfects, the transvaluation of single events. His stories of Mary, events in Bethlehem and Nazareth, vignettes of childhood, all of which lead up to the climax in Jerusalem, and the even more far-flung pivots of the tale—from Jerusalem and Galilee, to Antioch, Samaria, Caesarea, Gaza, Egypt and thence westward through Cyprus, Asia, Greece, Malta to Rome —become in his hand a spiritual map, rich in colour, but held together by the framework of divine Providence.

The harmony of the whole and the disharmony of finely observed details constitute the literary triumph of this belief in an overarching Providence. The Acts of the Apostles could so easily have proved abortive in failure. Its fragmentation—of places and people—could have produced not a story but a string of unrelated events. But the spiritual mastery of the author lifts them from their chaotic atomism into a harmonious whole, whose underlying principle operates everywhere and at all times.

This vision of faith requires the greatest subtlety of presentation. The ancient world, as we have seen, bequeathed to the biblical writers a technique which was not only serviceable but also capable of complex development. Once the linear form had become established and the story-teller was expected to work in a large room with perspective, there was really no limit to what could be done in this field. The Hebrew narrative, it is true, seems at first to make little use of the wide range of the linear form. It spurns the employment of the subordinate phrase, and although a greater flexibility can be discerned as time goes on the main burden of the story rests on the direct indicative: 'And it came to pass...and it happened'. But, strangely enough, this indisputable lack of sophistication and elegance does not impede the narrator from achieving his effect. For example, the stories in Genesis do somehow create in us the illusion of the large area. Partly this is due to constant movement within the story—'and he arose', 'and he went', etc.—partly to the economy of the style and the particularly poignant use of dialogues within that economy. But perhaps it is precisely the given limitation of style which in the last resort establishes a certain order. The area in which we move is big enough, but not too big. It can admit characterization of individuals, such as David, certain kings, great prophets, but it does not allow them to dominate the story. This, as we have seen, is controlled by God. What is lacking on the horizontal plane may be said to be supplied on the vertical. Even Luke, who obviously works with a far larger area, not only in a topographical but also in a stylistic sense, adheres to the principle of limitation. His linguistic ability would enable him to vie with, and do better than, Josephus but he applies a deliberate control. Jesus, Peter, and Paul move and speak, but they do not burst the linear limitation.

This restraint belongs as much to the narrative as to the faith. The human contours are mostly drawn to show up the divine background. We noticed in our perusal how rarely we find an exhaustive treatment of character. Even Peter, whose denial in the Passion narrative certainly takes up a surprising amount of detailed treatment, is not nearly as well known as, say, Judas Maccabaeus, not to mention Socrates. But constant self-restraint, especially in the Gospels, makes room for the indescribable. It does not have to forgo the visual colouring in order to bring out the transcendent. Thus Luke's end to Acts, with the description of an ambush in Jerusalem and the long ill-fated voyage to Ostia, goes a long way towards secular reportage in vividness. Yet his self-imposed 'order' leaves the reader in no doubt that what is at stake are not the adventures of a few choice Christians but the over-arching and all-embracing providence of God.

The Hebrew genius for the narrative has an uncanny bent towards welding nearness to the action with distance to the spectator. The climactic events of the Exodus invariably reach us in this manner. We feel that the narrator is near the fire which Moses sees, follows the angel who brings destruction to the Egyptians, is part of the escaping party, witnesses the rebellions, etc.; but he mediates his story in such a way that we look at it from outside and from far off. This effect involves not direct participation but the perspective of faith. Similarly the Gospels transmute the direct witness into the assent of belief, and John states quite openly that his purpose of bearing testimony is to create faith. Perspective is to literature what faith is to spiritual apprehension.

This way of looking at people and events, both from nearby and from far off, in a single vision, enables the narrator to combine an intensity of feeling with a sense of relaxation. All the famous battle scenes and adventures in the historical books could be cited to make this point. A classical example in this type of composition is the story of David's triumph over Goliath. The narrator uses the single combat of tradition to illumine the whole area of conflict. The young lad opposes the giant, the unarmed wins over the heavily armoured. The style is overtly factual, but an intensity of feeling is obtained by the forward movement of the narrative. The spectator cannot help being anxious. He identifies with the brave, the young, the beautiful. Unwittingly he sides with him, and thus with his trust in Yahweh. When at last the giant's head is severed and the armour stripped off the corpse, there is a David in everyone. Yet, at the same time, this identification, which absorbs all sorts of aggressive passions, is played out against a relaxed background which cools the passion. The enjoyment of the story is precisely vouchsafed by the roominess of the stage, which gives the spectator a chance to breathe in a state of happy detachment.

The intentions of the Gospels are less easily defined. Mark proclaims his evangel in too clipped a style to give much roominess and air, although even he makes exceptions, as in the case of the two stories about miraculous feeding of multitudes. Matthew and John similarly never appear to make any concession to the building up of perspective. Their polemical directness would seem to exclude the possibility of relaxation, although, strangely enough, many readers find the Johannine soliloquies essentially consolatory. But the Jesus of these Gospels is never anything but transcendental. When he prays, acts, indicts, and suffers there is no roominess behind or beyond the central figure. Hence the faith is also essentially two-dimensional, Jesus between God and Man.

Luke, however, takes us away from this claustrophobic

centre. Right from the start he handles the birth narrative with a freedom which Matthew could not tolerate. The material has an independent life because the narrator opens for the listener a third dimension. The whole wide world is present. Luke increases the intensity of personal feeling because he moves within the cosmic vastness. Thus the portrayal of Jesus is not diminished but enhanced through Luke's so-called humanism. In Acts the spaciousness becomes even more pronounced, partly because the main characters are always in motion, but partly also because the narrator gives his work a note of enjoyment and relaxation. By doing so he transforms the nature of faith imperceptibly and fundamentally. He begins the giant stride from narrow polemics, sectarian existence, and eschatological foreshortening of time, towards the universal and acceptable religion of empire. We are on the threshold of a new culture.

22 Erosion and Collapse

The new culture in the Hellenistic Roman world became Christian largely through the influence of the biblical narrative, precisely because it was not considered, or meant to be enjoyed, as literature. The Church's emphasis on action—the 'Do this!' of its liturgy—ruled out even the biblical tradition of taking a story as just that. Further stories were not admitted into the canon of Scripture labelled sacred. In the context of the Church's affirmation of the Christian life as opposed to pagan ways the narrative suffered a sea-change. The Gospels, in particular, were not simply retold to remember past miracles and to stipulate codes of behaviour, but to challenge the world. They became a power to transform the Roman Empire and the human scene. But this epoch-making success gave to the Church not only power as the trustee of the Scriptures. The question of meaning could not be suppressed. In the absence of new authoritative narratives, commentaries on the Gospels, for example, had to fulfil the needs of growing communities. Even giants like Augustine, whose literary genius reached the whole civilized world in his *Confessions*, did not write a story of God but commented on many books of the Bible. As among the Jews, so for the Christians, the commentary replaces the narrative.

The Christians faced a task which proved more daunting than that confronting the Jews. Over the centuries the genius of Judaism absorbed the story *(Haggadah)* within the vast legal corpus *(Halakhah)*. But somehow the new Testament narrative could never become a 'way of life' and take second place to teaching. This does not mean that it was not tried; after all, the Christian teacher found his precedent already in the Old Testament, where, for example, the Priestly editor could spoil the Balaam tradition by turning the comedy of the prophet, who must learn from the talking ass, into a humourless story of an arch-villain whom the Moabites employ against Israel (cf. Num. 22—4 with ch. 31).

The attempt to 'explain' a story by ironing out its contradictions is reflected in many Christian commentaries. Not only Balaam's ass but countless other episodes evoked the desire to harmonize events in retrospect. Uncomfortable difficulties raised by, say the binding of Isaac or the raising of Lazarus, could not escape the attention of cultured exegetes, such as Clement and Origen. If the story was to validate its claims to being 'inspired' how could it at the same time exhibit contradictions or highly improbable features? Where reason protests against fantasy the commentator has a tough job and contrives a method which seeks spiritual truth at the expense of historical realism.

The vigour of the stories and the sharp edges of their characters fortunately defeated the lures of complete allegorizing. Even mere moralizing would not do to accommodate the behaviour of Balaam or Abraham or Jacob. The Antiochene school took a stand against allegorizing and resisted the abuses of spiritual interpretation. David remained David instead of becoming merely a shoot of the stem of Jesse leading up to Christ. John the Baptist was not yet reduced to a mere pointer to Jesus. For a time the Gnostic disdain for earthly realism even heightened the Christians' esteem for their 'simple' stories. They were not philosophy and not meant to be Gnostic symbols.

Nevertheless, the centralization of power in the Church, itself heir to Roman imperialism, could not but affect the place of the story and its interpretation. It was aimed at uniformity and thereby curtailed the freedom of interpretation. Less room remained for the polarities inherent in all good narratives. The patterning of power in the Church also rubbed off on the treatment of tradition. Contradictions become insufferable. The Church defends and formulates her faith by, and against, men trained in logic and rhetoric. Even the great Greek and Latin masters of exegesis, such as Chrysostom and Augustine, display a certain impatience with their beloved Bible just at the point when the story becomes intriguingly difficult. Only Jerome seems to cherish the text just as it stands with all its open questions.

Perhaps it would not go too far to see a connection between this drying up of the creative Word and the disasters of the Christian East and West. Histories, such as Eusebius', and lives of the saints and accounts of martyrdom, could not recapture the illumination and inspiration of the biblical narrative. The Lukan model, which is for us the high point of traditional story-telling, shows up the weakness of so much later writing. The Christian Fathers prove by the absence of genius that it cannot be produced at will. The use of an earthly and heavenly vocabulary by itself achieves very little. To talk of pigs and angels does not create the Lukan dimension.

Nevertheless the Biblical narrative lay dormant as in a seed-bed during the Dark Ages in the West. It was recited and it was acted upon in communities. It evoked illustrations and ornamentations. At the first dawn of Europe's awakening the story-teller waits again in the wings. The Christian narrator resumes his task to express and nourish the faith. The Gospel pattern and especially the Lukan heaven-and-earth perspective no longer act as a brake but as a stimulant. A Bede assumes that the earthly history corresponds to a higher order of reality. These tentative beginnings usher in a great resurgence in the age of cathedrals, universities, schools, hospitals, missions, etc. Their foundations stem from the narrative—e.g. the Good Samaritan—translated into the Here and Now.

The medieval model combined the vertical or transcendental with the horizontal or immanent. God walked in the medieval Garden as in the Paradise myth. The tomb of Christ was empty and the stone rolled away as in the Gospel tradition. Yet this apparent simplicity was inseparable from the vast complexity of the whole bustling life on earth and the complex cosmology and philosophy. The Gothic cathedrals with their springing vaults and flying buttresses embody the strain and contradictions of a culture which acted out the paradox of faith. Already there are signs that the actual experience on earth and the faith deposit of the narrative are locked in tension. But this tension is still creative.

The narrative then, becomes enshrined in the form of poetry. For Dante, for example, the whole earthly existence, in Florence, before A.D. 1300, recapitulates the mythological and biblical narratives. The pattern of the Old and New Testaments stands in a direct relationship to man in his corporate life and in his free individuality. The human phenomenon, as presented in the Divine Comedy, cannot be separated from the whole model of the universe. Dante thus forges again the Great Chain of Being, and the narrative of God and Christ and Holy Spirit questions, and answers to, the human condition in its totality. The realism of the present, therefore, is anchored in the reality of God. The Florentine masters, who paint Annunciations, Birth, Adorations and Crucifixions against a Tuscan and Umbrian background, depict the presence of Jesus in Italy.

The tension between horizontal reality and vertical tradition can still be seen at its most creative in art and architecture, and heard at its most impressive in the music from the Venetians to the baroque masters. These great accomplishments testify to an ever increasing strain. The Christian narrative lives in windows, sculptures, and decorative art, but it no longer connects organically with the dawning world of science and reason. Dante himself is a prey to the pull in two directions and castigates himself for relying on reason rather than revelation. Yet his genius allows him to weave the secular tale into his heavenly order. After him the erosion of the biblical narrative pattern as part of life grows apace. The wave of secularization cannot be arrested. The princes of the Renaissance no longer view their achievements and failures in the mirror of salvation history. A Titian paints the secular as distinct from the sacred, and soon the world is a stage where men live and die as if there were no other tale to tell. Curiously enough, the Reformation is an attempt to put the clock back, to rule Geneva, for example, as if it were Jerusalem, or to sail to the new world as if it were the promised land. The Reformed churches re-open the Bible for the people in the conviction that the Word, and with it the story, is apart from time and space, and therefore for all time and space. But the age of Reason scorns the attempt, for example in Gibbon's mocking words: 'How shall we excuse the supine inattention of the Pagan and philosophic world to these evidences which were presented by Omnipotence?' When Hardy quotes this accusation, more than a century later in *Jude the Obscure*, these 'evidences' have been found wanting in efficacy on a broad front.

This cynical dismissal of these literary evidences seems to ignore wilfully the amazing and lasting achievements of the Christian tradition. It brushes aside in a cavalier fashion the whole European culture which still brings a coherent picture out of the centrifugal forces of the modern age. Yet it must be admitted that the tensions and polarities no longer yielded to the optimistic earth-heaven, man-god correspondence as conveyed in simple narratives. It is not an accident that the genius of writers engages in their creative struggle by the use and development of poetical forms. Just as the extremely complicated polyphony of the sixteenth century and thereafter manifests a triumph of order over disorder so also the literary forms are made to serve the unrest, doubt, and power of the new civilization. Prose fails where the complexity of verse succeeds. The narrative—starting in the Middle Ages—is itself converted into an epic or play. The story still dominates the whole but its style of telling amounts to a transformation. *Paradise Lost* could not have been written in prose. Poetry is not just a certain mannerism to preserve the Christian pattern, as if to patch over the cracks of a failing faith, but the necessary means of unifying the irreconcilable polarities which beset man. The poetic forms alone seem adequate to serve the pluralistic and fragmentary burden of the new age. Their success underlines the erosion of the traditional forms of faith. A Bunyan may seem to arrest this erosion. His *Pilgrim's Progress* demonstrates the hidden resources which the biblical narrative still offers to the genius who accepts the traditional pattern of belief. He keeps the door open, but there are few who can follow him.

The break-down of the faith and the narrative go hand in hand. It is not concerned with detail, such as disbelief in specific episodes in the narrative. The unification of polarities, which we regard as the outstanding characteristic of the Christian pattern, no longer commands the assent of an educated class. It suspends belief in the form of things as presented by Luke-Acts (to take the most extreme instance). Some readers may still share the existentialist understanding of Paul, as in Galatians and Romans, but they shirk the physical-metaphysical, optimistic-providential, human-divine harmony, which begins in Genesis and culminates in Acts. On the one hand, modern scientific theories contradict the 'pre-established harmony'; on the other, human experiences clash with the framework of a benevolent providence. Where, say the critics, are the angels who open prisons? The narrative is open to scorn and derision, unless it is stylized in, and 'privileged' as, poetry.

Notwithstanding this repudiation of the Christian pattern an inner dialect ties even the most eloquent agnostic to the tradition. Increasingly men, out of sympathy with the Christian faith, translate the Christian claims. Goethe and Schiller, for example, cannot simply revert to paganism nor be content with the secular rationalism or moralism of their age. In plays and poetry they come to terms with a lost heritage. Goethe's Faustus can receive a redemption on the Christian pattern despite the total abolition of the claims of the Gospel. Dante's Heaven is still open, with Mary and the saints, though the faith of Dante is abandoned. But this could not have been accomplished in prose. Only the play with its infinite range of poetical forms could contain the new cosmic dimension.

The collapse of the Christian narrative in prose is not sudden nor complete. Yet the miraculous rise of the European novel owes little to the Christian tradition, except that the men and women who come to figure in episodic tales and adventures still live in towns and villages with churches and parsons and the inherited speech of Christian customs. Hardy is perhaps the greatest representative of generations of writers who live by the tradition which they repudiate. He cannot lament the malign hand of the celestial despot without alluding constantly to the biblical heritage. His creations are in a sense a protest against the vanishing of the old world of cosmic coherence. Henchard, Mayor of Casterbridge, ought to be forgiven, rewarded, and guided like the prodigal son or the victim who fell among thieves. But, alas, the ancient springs have dried up. The woman taken in adultery was forgiven, but Tess must be executed. The ancient symmetry is lost, and the principle of incongruity rules where once coherent correspondence made sense of human suffering. Hardy still seeks to accomplish the unification of polarities despite the absence of God and a benign providence, and because he makes these moral demands upon himself and opposes the meaningless and painful fragmentation of life, he and his readers connect with the biblical forms of faith. But the connection is more like a spasm of despair. It negates what it would like to affirm.

Not all the prose of the age went this courageous way. Indeed, the main stream of novels became a support for the masses and was designed to meet the needs of the market in which consolidation through reading was priced highly. But for the most part these novels, whether they circulated in the salons of the rich or reached the poor in instalments, no longer touch upon our theme. They resolved the tensions of life without invoking the dimensions of faith. Church-going and prayer may still give a religious flavour to many of these stories, which proliferated in Western Europe and America during the nineteenth century, but in whatever context they occur they have ceased to belong to the divine comedy. The comedy, like the tragedy, is human, of this world, here and now.

Yet even in this secular age the story of Christ himself makes its impact as a literary phenomenon. Lives of Christ begin to appear in an avalanche of either pietistic reaction to secularism, or as an accommodation to it. There are as many imaginary lives of Christ as there are pictures of Jesus. They vary from the reverential retelling of the Saviour's life to a free fictional portrayal of a Son of Man. Jesus becomes the fulcrum of all sorts of projections. We seem to be on the threshold not only of the restoration of the Christ figure, but also of the prose narrative as the rightful medium for the portrayal of the faith. But, in fact, the vast output only confirms the collapse of the tradition, for although some of these stories are readable and even excellent literature they contradict the Christian pattern. Even the mere sentimentalizing of the Gospel story, as in endless Sunday School books, breaks unconsciously with the tradition. We can only marvel that the candy-floss of sugary Jesus religion and the moralizing of cautionary Christ tales could have created a passing culture which only ended with the First World War. The anticipation of this catastrophe and its consequences changed the direction of the lives of Christ.

But the persistence of the Christ figure extended beyond the range of both pietistic lives and scientifically reconstructed lives of Jesus. Fictional transfigurations of the Big Fisherman reached the market to further the erosion of the traditional pattern. These portrayals were no longer of Jesus himself, as he had been or was supposed to have been, but of some fictional character who was endowed with Christ-like features. They were, in fact, not unrelated to the hagiography of ancient times. Lives of the Saints and Martyrs, whether factual or imaginary, had shown traces of the Christlike character. The *imitatio Christi* had governed chronicles, such as Bede's, and romantic tales as told of St Francis and his followers. But these stories still reflected the Christian pattern of the heaven-earth correspondence, though they did not stress the cosmic motif. The modern transfigurations turn inward, even when the author, such as Dostoevsky, seeks to connect the orthodox faith with the contemporary problems. His *Idiot*, perhaps the most influential novel of the Christ-carrying hero, is a marvellous rendering of the innocent, non-violent, suffering, and wholly isolated Redeemer figure in a world of guilt, violence, cruelty, and mob organization. Prince Myshkin not only unites these polarities, as in the Gospel tradition, but carries them within himself. So far the transformation is wholly successful. But Dostoevsky cannot help breaking with the triumphalism of the tradition, for the hero is caught and shut up in the world which he does not conquer. He withdraws at the end, just as he arrives at the beginning. The railway lines which lead into, and out of, the capital symbolize the claustrophobic centre from which there is no other escape.

The 'Prince Christ' is the 'good man' of moral beauty and a presence which impresses all those who come into contact with him. But he is sick and perhaps even mad. He is the outsider and belongs neither to this earth nor to the heaven of God. He is the enthusiast and depressive at once, totally incapable of coming to terms with the harsh climate of modern times. Yet in a curious way his impact through fiction is probably greater than that of all the lives of the Nazarene. But he also irritates the reader. Dostoevsky himself remedied this defect when he created subsequently the figure of Alyosha Karamazov, who is made to leave the monastery and work in the world. Moreover, it was Dostoevsky's intention to expose Alyosha fully to the sinfulness of this world, so that he, the great sinner, could at length become the great genuine redeemer. No one can fail to respond to this transfiguration of Jesus in Alyosha. This response is partly fuelled by the romantic longing and the dramatic suspense which gives a modern, and yet also traditional context, to the unfolding of the story. Moreover, the vastness of the canvas and the eschatological fervour (Alyosha among the boys), the realism of the suffering of the innocent (Dmitri) and the poor (the Captain), and the humour and lightness of touch (the scenes at the monastery, the debauched buffoon of a father), bring a Lukan flavour to the whole. But even Dostoevsky cannot salvage the cosmic coherence of the pattern. In *Crime and Punishment* Sonja can read the Raising of Lazarus to the murderer Raskolnikov, and *The Devils* work out their destruction under the motto of the story of Legion, yet Resurrection and Descent into Hell do not transcend this world. The story and the faith do not deny the cosmic dimension, the heaven-earth correspondence, and the coherence of the parts in the whole of the divine design. The reader may affirm or remain neutral, as long as he is himself involved in the transformation.

Dostoevsky, however, stands on his own. His contemporary, Tolstoy, even came to doubt the validity of the whole enterprise of novel writing. The author of *War and Peace* who brought together a universe of polarities got bored with, and even hated, the moral torpor which all fiction engenders. The reader wants to be titillated, not educated, let alone converted. He requires love stories, such as *Anna Karenina* (rightly described as the story of human love to end all love stories), to be entertained. Even if he identifies with the characters and suffers with them, he can and will turn the pages and close the book, unreformed. Tolstoy underestimates perhaps our experience, as we react to Karenin's frigidity, Vronsky's passion, and Anna's total disenchantment. Are we really unchanged as we follow her along the railway track, despairing of an adulterous love which has grown stale, and desiring only to be crushed by the engine and the trucks? Is not this suicidal impulse the prelude to the Gospel of repentance? Tolstoy, however, in spite of writing *Resurrection* many years after, expressed disgust with art because the profoundest aesthetic experience does not reform motives and conduct. As Levin meditates at the end of *Anna Karenina*, so Tolstoy judges about himself and all men: 'This new feeling has not changed me'. Admittedly, life will not be meaningless as before and every action will be invested with meaning, but —contrast of all contrasts—Levin will not only still have rows, waste time, be alienated from his wife, but he will also fail to attain to the perfection of the Kingdom of God. Perfection is the damning word, taken from the Gospels, and given, in Tolstoy's critique of literature, the threatening voice of total condemnation. Morality has lost its context.

This breaking-up of tradition accelerates after Tolstoy and is hastened by war and revolution. The favourite transfigurations of Jesus pursue a humanitarian, socialist portrayal of *The Saint*. Modernist leanings and Christian socialist tracts find their outlet in novels and films, in which the good priest (Spencer Tracy) leads the community by example. But the engaging naivety of this outlook simply could not stand up against the seriousness of post-war problems. The cynicism of a disillusioned generation welcomed the anticlerical milieu of the *Good Soldier Schweik*, where the priest is simply the tool of the exploiting class and Christian morality itself is only a cloak for private gain. Comrade Jesus is either a confidence trickster in whatever representative he comes before us, or he is himself a dupe of the social and economic forces which enslave all. The Communist leader is thought to be more effective in the liberation of the oppressed than the passive idealist Jesus whose crucifixion may stand as a warning against erroneous strategy. Curiously enough, the lines between Party and Church cross more often than one would expect. The socialist novel also has its themes of initiation, tests, disputes, treacheries, common meals, imprisonments, executions. Water, bread and wine, blood and tears, unite the new with the old by a thread. But the total framework has vanished. Even where the ancient ritual and symbolism still play a part the Gospel lives on by parody rather than in imitation.

Socialist slogans, the shouts of the mob, the protesters' abuse, the repetitive shrieks of pop groups, the sex-and-drug happenings, may still invoke some lost strand of the story of Jesus, but they cannot confront us with anything but a parody of the narrative. This is not only due to political propaganda and ideological opposition. The media offer neither time nor space to the disclosure of the plot, the growth of character, the different dimensions of feeling, and the working out of polarities within a coherent design. Impressions are conveyed in jerky stabs. The formless, rather than the formal, meets the immediate demands of a disintegrating society. High volumes of sound, intensity of light, an unprecedented velocity of sequences, produce an irrational, excessive, and dissonant fragmentation, which blinds and deafens the human senses. This formlessness corresponds not to the coherent structure of a moral universe, but to the empty void of all. The street crowded with traffic and leading nowhere in particular symbolized the break with the great tradition. It seems almost like the end of the story.

23 *The rebirth of narrative*

The crisis of the story is the crisis of faith. Our culture, obsessed by trivialities here and now, to the total exclusion of the there and then, has lost its centre of gravity outside itself. Thus the modern story contrasts with the classical models in their great variety. It mutilates the universe we live in. The Lukan proportions, for example, no longer operate in the claustrophobic prison of waste land, where faceless men strip themselves or others for torture and execution. Hunger, sickness, and death no longer pertain to an architectural design, which offers release into distance and infinity. In this world people live and die alone. They may articulate streams of consciousness, but they do not meet others whom they affect or by whom they are affected. In the classical range of stories speech not only affirms or negates facts but changes people and their plight. The speaking Jesus, for example, is met by questioning demons, opposing enemies, beseeching victims, and bewildered disciples. The words which pass create a new reality which binds all to each. The modern dialectic, in contrast, heightens the gulf which separates all from each.

This claustrophobic universe can only be resolved from within. External events as such do not penetrate to its core of inertia. Science fiction, for example, which certainly opens up the material universe, with the aid of the informed imagination, yields singularly little in the release of the imprisoned mankind. On the contrary, the rebirth of the story has already begun in a different manner. Old and new literary forms combine to map out the pursuit of the centre of gravity which, though within, lies also outside.

The pursuit of this target uses ancient themes in a wholly modern guise. The writer questions our human destiny in order to exorcise the fragmentation into nothing. He concentrates on the inner state to sound the polarities of the whole creation. Thus the centre of gravity within is made to correspond to that without. In this interlocking universe the groans of the whole creation articulate the need for redemption. The intensity of feeling, though stated in a detached and cool manner, gives birth to the story which pinpoints the cosmic dilemma in the life of the individual.

Franz Kafka, whose output is small enough (and mostly unfinished) to serve as an example, enters this world of tradition without sounding in the least traditional. This Jew of Prague, writing in German and nurtured in law, literature, and religion, stands at the crossroads for our century. He and his stories represent our search for identity and security in a world which denies us both. In his late story 'The Burrow' he dreams of the old utopia of the perfect state, the 'mighty fortress', the indestructible peace. But the dream is shattered by the impossibility of such a state. The animal burrows accordingly in vain, for even complete seclusion would not yield security but only the real threat, namely that of the existence of the self. From this there is never an escape. Even the 'Construction of the great Wall of China' (another fragment), if universalized, cannot fill all the gaps of our vulnerable defences. It may be better than the Tower of Babel, but it only stresses the hopelessness of our task. As long as *We* construct the gaps remain—ourselves.

Hence, following Kafka's basic insight, what is needed is change. The alienation of the self could end if the self were to transform itself. But for Kafka metamorphosis is no panacea at all, in as much as it is forced upon us against our will. In the story 'The Metamorphosis' the wretched business-man Gregor Samsa becomes a beetle, which puts an end to his work. He wants to 'forget it', but 'it' has happened to him and he cannot shake 'it' off as a bad dream. The transformation into a verminous insect is the seal upon his ego, the potential made actual. He cannot return to his former state and must endure the gradual eclipse of himself. His transformation contrasts with the store of legends and fairy stories in which the hero becomes a better, worthier man after passing through the animal state. He is no Pinnochio or goose-boy Nils (S. Lagerloeff), whose adventures end in the safe return and self-knowledge. In this modern tragedy of metamorphosis neither the hero, nor the reader, are purged with pity and terror.

Yet something else happens. The victim's degradation is not confined to himself. He becomes an embarrassment to his relations, for whom he has worked loyally in the past. His sister loves him. Yet the family cannot tolerate the beetle's presence. The bug cannot be isolated, for the shame of its existence affects father, mother, sister, servants, and colleagues. In his humiliation he has a power over them which they cannot break, except by crushing him. The beetle must be thrown away—dead. But this physical event is the result of a spiritual death which is not confined to the victim. The beetle has established links, and these relationships adumbrate the metamorphosis. The single event has created new and demanding possibilities, and the crushing of the beetle opens a multi-dimensional spectrum which now confronts us.

The worm of Kafka's ordeal resembles that of the worm Israel in the prophetic tradition. It also seeks a centre of gravity outside the process of degradation. The crushed and the worthless are ready for another metamorphosis. This story of perdition has no happy ending, but it evokes a longing for new life. It is a lamentation in prose, which, like Mark's Gospel, ends on a note of mourning and fear. But the lamentation itself is proof that the beetle may be 'changed', and with it the guilty who assented to 'the final solution'.

Kafka's *America* resumes the quest for salvation in the traditional field of the long journey. He recalls for us not only the explorations of Gilgamesh and the ventures of Odysseus, or the journeys of Paul and all the mariners who sailed the seas, but also the thousands of miserable, but expectant, groups which crowded the transatlantic boats in ever increasing numbers, seeking to make their fortunes, getting away from persecutions or bad reputations, and often failing after their arrival in the new world. Karl in America is thus representative of man's utopian endeavour which seems on the surface wholly given over to practical concerns, and yet always embodies the flight from the known evils to an unattained good. For this purpose Kafka can use the traditional form of episodic story-telling, which takes the reader from the boat and its confined cabins, to the mansion of the rich uncle in New York, and thence to a questionable half-built house in the country, and finally across the country to the as yet legendary Oklahoma. Again, in the traditional manner, the passenger becomes the guest of the rich, the outcast and vagrant among the poor, the victim of the ruthless, and at last the pilgrim who is sustained by an inner energy which focuses upon a hope yet to be realized. Yet Kafka once again transforms the story, not by allegorizing, but by sharpening its outlines. Karl's needs are wholly contemporary, and the ship's crew, the uncle's household, the tricksters, the inns and their routine, the mobs and publicity men, are like an etching of life in America in 1910. The women too, though rooted in the tradition of Homer and the Bible, are real dolls, temptresses, and domineering mothers. The stage is indeed crowded with actors, but their impact does not lessen the solitude of Karl, whose pilgrimage universalizes the eternal quest, embodied now in the passage from a European port to Oklahoma, and always evoking that from earth to heaven. Karl is 'the man who was lost sight of' (Kafka's original title of the novel), for better or for worse.

The pursuit of the ideal breaks off abruptly within sight of the fantastic open-air 'nature' theatre in Oklahoma. It symbolizes the promised land with a welcome to all, but there always remains the undercurrent of a threatening ambiguity. The external world reflects the deception of the inward state, the polarity between the essential person and the existential reality. Hence, for Kafka, judgement is implicit in our destiny. The pleas and counterpleas of tradition, the accusations and protestations of the innocent, the necessity of bringing and hearing a case, turn his modern world into a court. In a short story *The Judgment* he subjects his hero Georg to the punishment of suicide, forced upon him by the love for parents and a friend, which he has, or is alleged to have, abused. He returns to this theme time and again and consummates all the contradictions of our time and the human psyche in his *Trial*. Here all escape hatches, of boats and unknown continents, are stopped, for the *Dies Irae* of tradition has come again. But the books which are opened and the witnesses who are called and the legal authorities who officiate remain as ambiguous as in the trial of the Son of Man. This trial is the inevitable case of humanity, caught between the predictably certain machinery of an unstoppable procedure and its innate need for self-justification, acquittal, approbation, and freedom.

The trial of Joseph K. continues thus the revelation on the dimensions which we know from the Bible. The ordinariness of the arrest, the complications of the hearings, the void of empty court rooms, the friendliness of some, the hostility of others, the eyes of the peering neighbours, the cruelty of men employed in the security forces, the echelons of rank within the judiciary, the fears and hopes of the accused, the reactions of the family, build up a formidable backcloth of historical realism and even prophetic insight into things to come. But this 'lower' world, with its inexorable logic, corresponds to a 'higher' order which we know in dreams and of which all trials bear vestiges.

K.'s trial is not a transfiguration of the trial of Jesus, nor a pietistic echo or a modernistic parody. It articulates quite simply the truth that man is on trial, not because he is brought to it from outside, on charges which may or may not be trumped up, but because he puts himself on trial. Life is an ordeal, and modern man is caught within the coils of the machine. Kafka writes several decades before the perfection of electronic spying or recording devices, but having worked in an insurance office he is already sensitive to the dehumanizing process which operates by numbers, statistics, filing systems, dossiers and endless officialdom. The trial, which he at first resists, become K.'s obsessional need, for in no other way can he establish his identity. The polarity between innocence and guilt makes up his real self. He seeks the trial and does not run away.

In this novel the whole Christian pattern of the trial is reborn without a hint of imitation. In the devious course of justice nothing is gained. The procedural comedy entangles all in an apocalyptic confusion, though every scene is rendered with perfect clarity. The tussle between light and darkness is once again a potent force in an unending drama. K.'s reliance on advocacy from outside ends in failure, for the lawyer Huld (= Grace) is ill and altogether untrustworthy. As K. severs his connection with the advocate and stands on his own feet he approaches the climax. It lies beyond law, ill-grace (perverted and weak), and procedural techniques. In the Cathedral K. receives the illumination that the court wants nothing from him, and that he was free to enter and leave the sacred halls of justice. But the priest in the dark Cathedral offers his comfort, if such it is, too late. 'The readiness is all'—but K. was not ready. The accused goes to his ritualistic execution, to be stabbed and throttled, like a dog.

The trial spans the polarity of life and death. It transcends criminal indictments and civil torts and takes us back to Mount Moriah and Golgotha, as well as forward to the final assault, the penetration of the many recesses, the corridors and chambers, through which the goal must at length be reached. Kafka does not set acquittal as the end, but full acceptance in communion. In *The Castle* the ordeal of K. evokes all the striving of the mystics' active passion, and passive suffering, for unity. The land-surveyor arrives on a snowy evening in the unknown village. How can he be permitted to settle down and be accepted among the community which is itself controlled by the unknown powers at the Castle? Who rules at the Castle? How can the ramifications of power be reached?

What is the way into the bureaucracy which conceals what it could reveal? Can anyone be trusted? Innkeepers, peasants, teachers, barmaids, servants of all sorts, cobblers, boys and girls, stand out in relief from the darkness. They also depend upon the Castle and their reactions to K. are governed by their own status in the complex mechanism. Nothing is quite what it seems. K. cannot enter the community as if it had no past. He releases the past by his presence and it is not to his advantage. Successes are short-lived, such as temporary accommodations, and even love, engagement, and the promise of marriage, are but the prelude to an ever-diminishing chance of acceptance. Every advantage gained is cancelled by disadvantages for the future. The advance, as on a chess-board, is illusory. The Castle, barely visible, and never accessible, drains the applicant of all strength. Inaction, silence, disappearance, weakness, error, duration, distance, slow down, impede, and halt every endeavour in the heavy snow. K. cannot help deviating as he waits for signals. In this empire of secretaries and their bundles of paper progress is impossible.

Where the Christian tradition surrounded the striving pilgrim with ghostly enemies, with lions, leopards, bears, and other beasts to attack him in the woods, held up by stinking moats, and frightened by eerie sounds of owls, Kafka dispenses with the fantastic, which is still found so often in contemporary art and literature (Tolkien, Peake). The pilgrim battles with the world of permits and the procedural routine, a nightmarish chaos, which is ordered with the utmost precision, an unmitigated evil, which stands above all censure, an enclosed entity which sucks all life into itself. Investigations, minutes, checks, party instructions, reports, memoranda, and retrieval systems, data-banks, wind like convolvulus, or others weeds, their strangling stems and feeders into the living soil of community. Drained of the life-blood it loses its solidity and instead of free and mutual support all seek to feed on each. How can K. enter the Castle?

The modern narrative has no overt moment of vindication.

Yet Kafka places the new life in the area of the improbable and the impossible. At the end of the trial the self-condemned sees lights in the windows and even the outline of shapes: could they be the signal of friendship? Could the peering and inquisitive eyes of the past change into sympathetic messengers? The potential of redemption is there. As one official, encountered by chance in *The Castle*, declares during the nightly interview: the rare possibility exists, when the incredible happens, when total despair yields to utter felicity, when one word, one gesture, one glance of trust undoes the whole structure of power.

This is the moment of recognition, which used to be called faith. At such a time the accused finds justice because he has the courage to be; the impostor, who would get into the Castle by false pretences, ceases from the absurd and doomed invasion of power. His death from exhaustion permits him to 'die unto sin', to 'forget', washed in the waters of Lethe. Death no longer stands for termination but serves as the threshold. Neither acquitted in the trial, nor rewarded for all his applications and calculations to gain the coveted foothold in the Castle, the accused is given the unexpected and the pilgrim the improbable: Grace within, a total correspondence which binds his internal destiny to the whole cluster of stars. But, as at the end of Mark's Gospel, these things are suggested, felt, led up to: they cannot be proved.

They can even be disputed. Kafka's tales, none of which would have seen the light of day if the author's will had been respected, already receive widely varying comments from all sides. Like biblical literature, Kafka's work invites, nay compels, polarity of comment, since its very content lives by polarity. For some the evil of the Castle, the land-surveyor's dubious credentials, the finality of the execution, the will-o'-the-wisp of hope, the mirage of a helping hand, and the inexorable laws of the chess board, spell out a predetermined fragmentation of effort. For them the quest and the trial can only lead to the extinction of K. Others, however, (among

them Camus and Thomas Mann) espy Grace in the framework of the total abolition of Grace. Thus the modern narrative throws out the challenge of faith and doubt.

But we are not merely concerned with Kafka and the great
modern authors, whose work reaches this open-ended possibility of Grace, simply because their heroes, pilgrims, and
victims seem to demand it. They alert us to the dimension of
hope because their formal structure authenticates such a faith,
even if the claustrophobic universe, in which their heroes move,
does not. The polarity between men and women in their
struggle as persons, and the world in which they must live,
recalls, but does not owe anything to, the New Testament. It
is simply the reality of alienation which has never left us.
Kafka's K. wants to have an abiding city, a sure refuge, in
which, like a badger, he can make himself safely at home.
Mann's Hans Castorp wants to make *The Magic Mountain*
his home, a kind of haven for the sickness and decadence and
violence and yearning, which his generation came to fight out
on the battlefields. But they have here no abiding city, no
security, no real roots. Yet being un-rooted and outside the
safety of the communal warmth they find, as strangers, a
dimension beyond *ennui* and demonic destruction. The form
of the story contrasts the claustrophobic with the wide open
spaces beyond. The geographical contours correspond to the
spiritual plight. Just as Job's heap of dust outside the community eventually leads up to the immeasurable vastness of the
constellations, so the narrator also spans his canvas from the
miserable speck on the map to the unending globe.

Modern narrators, who attempt the conquest of meaningless
fragmentation, use to this end a wide range of styles. Kafka
places his narrative in an unspecified past in which the hero
appears without any explanation. In this thinly disguised biographical kind of story the author speaks of the hero in the
third person. No one is likely to ask how he knows what he
is about to tell. The author assumes a stance of faith, which
the reader accepts. Kafka's identification with K. affects the

reader, so that he shares K.'s anguish and ordeal. Thus the direct style of the antique third-person narrative in the past can become the formal vehicle of a first-person experience in the present. The story—no longer of Caesar nor of Paul, but of our contemporary brother—can gather the fragments into a meaningful whole.

The most telling style to achieve this transformation is frankly cast in the first person. The so-called I-style of narrative has the further advantage that it blends immediacy with distance, leaving the reader with a choice of response. He may either sympathize with, or react against, the hero. He is both more involved and less implicated, for he gets to know the hero from within, but he is not obliged to side with him. The author can therefore play upon his public by presenting himself, without really disclosing his total history. Like a painter he transforms the figures and the landscape. This is what Goethe called *Dichtung und Wahrheit*, the strange amalgam of facts and their poetic interpretation. The I-style combines many levels of awareness, recalling the Hebrew tradition with its legal formula (e.g., Nehemiah's testament to posterity), the realism of the travelogue (e.g., the 'We' eye-witnesses in Acts), the satirical observations (e.g., Apuleius' *Golden Ass*), and, above all, the curious unspoken relationship with the reader.

Among the many voices from the past, however, Augustine's 'I' remains the most influential. In his *Confessions* he bequeathed a model to literature which is famous not only for its style but also for its purpose. He condemns himself in order to make room for God's justification. He presents himself in his awful egocentricity. He exacerbates through his example the hopelessly claustrophobic condition of man. The reader who follows the boy and the young man in North Africa is not even expected to like the narrator. On the contrary, Augustine means him to reject the young Augustine in his gratuitous escapades and inward destruction. As the 'I' sinks ever deeper into the morass of corruption the reader gets used to the double vision of one condemned and one condemning. This strange experience prepares him for the climax, the call *Tolle, lege* (Take up and read!), the near-desperate Augustine's hour of conversion, when he opens the New Testament at the end of chapter 13 of the Epistle to the Romans. The reader watches the prisoner's leap to freedom and feels that the 'I' also watches him to make his escape.

Confessions of events in the 'I'-style are not restricted to reportage but have the power of eliciting faith. The individual 'I' does not preach but surveys his life as a representative of humanity. Dante, for example, is the supreme example for the penitent, who integrates his 'story' into the vast poetical cosmology of *The Divine Comedy*. The 'I' is never lost sight of, from the suicidal beginnings in the dark wood to the ascent into heaven. Bunyan reverts to 'He' in a kind of biblical prose to show the progress of every oppressed pilgrim. The dividing line between 'I' and 'He' has become very thin.

In our time the 'I'-style of narrative or confession has become common and may serve purely secular goals. From Rousseau to the latest sensational gossip we derive a tradition of overt scepticism. The confessions of sinners invite the condonation of all failures. But there is also a type of secular confession, which results in an implicit act of faith. The ancient form may carry the contemporary substance of faith.

Proust's *A la recherche du temps perdu* is the outstanding model of the modern 'confession'. Proust stands within lost time both as penitent and sufferer, who desired, enjoyed, and heightened the experience of sin. All the perversities and absurdities of this experience—the endless shades of snobism, ambitions, reflections of power, affections and disenchantments —are filtered back through the 'I' of the unique Marcel. But, like his great predecessors, this remote eccentric is one of us, the universal 'I', who distills passing time through his act of remembrance so as to regain the timeless core. Like Augustine he 'remembers', and this act of memory is in itself an act of faith. The 'I' remembers to unmake the past and to set free the future.

The 'I'-style of narrative has reached a complexity unknown to Augustine, Dante, or Bunyan. Its psychological intensity is paired with a mordant wit which the modern situation demands. Dostoevsky had already added the spice of irony to his unfolding drama of *The Devils*. The unnamed narrator brings an almost innocent, enquiring, and bewildered role to the mad conspiracy around him. Thus the reader stands on the brink of the total moral collapse with both horror and laughter. As the scene of this collapse reaches its height in the twentieth century, with 'final solutions' of murder as an accepted political model, the narrator exploits the 'I'-style in an ever-increasing subtlety of manner. Thomas Mann attains to perfection in the disclosure of hell with a humorous irony. His *Doctor Faustus* recapitulates the traditional theme of demonic inspiration which causes men to strive after greatness and to fall into the abyss. The composer Adrian Leverkühn is cast in the part of the magician who, like Nietzsche, must with religious devotion make and keep the pact with his inward devil. Only this total dedication to the task, at the expense of comfort and affection, can achieve the apocalyptic goal. A new music thus conceived, is born, matures, as Germany and the whole civilized world aspires to world-dominion and the final peak—beyond good and evil. Mann's story could easily become a cautionary tale, a morality play, or just a plain political tract. But the I-style transforms the ingredients. A nice, somewhat humdrum, Catholic high-school teacher, acts as the biographer of his friend Leverkühn. As this worthy Zeitblom tells the story he adds a humanistic flavour to the apocalypse, a domestic boyhood and student background to the rootless nihilism, and an unconscious lack of understanding to his painful record of facts. Zeitblom (flowering of time, in English!) spans the world of polarities, and the reader stands in the middle, both moved and amused.

The 'I'-style not only becomes the ideal vehicle for expressing the basic polarities of life—individual and society, inward feeling and external events, nearness of event and distance from it, the particular and the universal—but it also comes to dominate the problem of passing time. True, in countless stories the 'I' merely links episodes, induces a happy acceptance of make-belief, sharpens the picture, and adds fun (as in Twain's *Huckleberry Finn*). The technique seems to grow out of the jottings in a diary, and there is not even the intention of defeating time. But the 'religious' use of the 'I' in the story exploits all these subtleties in order to transcend time, not by obliterating it, but by subordinating it to the eternal. Lewis Carroll's joke ('beat time') hints at the profundity of the quest. Proust's 'I' becomes the mediator between time and timelessness, because he, mother's darling, grandmother's treasure, the aunt's favourite, remembers innocence in the growing corruption of the budding flowers. Standing between illusion and reality, the 'I' becomes the universal man in his quest for a return to the past, and therefore a future beyond. The famous madeleine dipped in tea, the sight and smells around Combray, the sea at Balbec, the little tune of Vinteuil, act as literary sacraments of time lost, remembered, transposed, and perhaps regained.

The conquest of time cannot be established as a fact, but only be evoked as a possibility. Nor does it always end happily. Kafka's K. conquers time only by submitting to it in death. Mann's Dr Faustus' final spasms of madness symbolize that of a whole generation, lost in its obsessive grandeur and creativity. Mann's Faustus, unlike Goethe's, forfeits redemption and there are no rose petals in an angelic home-coming. Heaven and resurrection seem far away. Nevertheless, these chronicles of our time recreate the large room, peopled with crowds, locked in conflict, heading towards disaster, in the expectation of a turning-point. The dénouement pleads for another and victorious reality, even if the degree of faith cannot be measured. The reader is free to make his grave in a world on the brink of total annihilation, but he may also, through the narrator's 'I', stand beyond this grave—if only to tell the tale. The narrator, like the evangelist, proves by telling the tale that the word outlives the disaster.

This conquest of duration-time through literary form is not a mechanical affair but derives from the development of character and the growing complexity of relationships. The modern 'I', unlike the hero of the episodic novel, changes his identity. He cannot be portrayed like Jesus—the same yesterday, today, and tomorrow. He is not morally consistent like Isaiah or Jeremiah. His polarities exceed the temperamental ups and downs of the disciples of Christ, who oscillate between fear and courage. In the Scriptures there is a remarkable absence of duality, whereas the contemporary hero always struggles with at least two, and often more, hearts in his breast. The experience of life corrupts and purges him, and he approaches death as 'another man' in a community which he has forged. He resembles Moses, tested in the ordeal of the desert. Passionate and frigid at the same time, he rules and is ruled like David.

The conquest of time is commensurate with the mutation of character enforced by time. Proust's Marcel cannot revert to innocence except through the floods of experience. He suffers, but it is not enough to describe and accept the suffering as the stuff of life; the modern novelist probes the motivation behind the changes and the destructive urges which cause them. The author's task, as Thomas Mann saw it, is to open the ancient well and to fill our empty buckets with the waters of the past. The old myths yield the healing springs which may irrigate the parched fields.

This task annuls the labours of up-dating the original stories ('making it relevant'). Proust does not re-tell the fall of Sodom and Gomorrah, but the story of the Cities of the Plain mirrors the bored violence which perverts Marcel's world. The present also reflects the patterns of antiquity, as in the elaborate structure of Joyce's *Ulysses*. We are in Dublin, but we hear echoes from around Ithaca. Mann does not re-tell the stories of

Genesis in his monumental trilogy *Joseph and his Brethren,* but he gives an eternal perspective to our mental and spiritual turmoil by means of these stories. The questionable nature of election, mission, humiliation, and vindication binds the past to the present, for Joseph is our man, his vanity endangers us, his rise and fall and rise typify our strange destiny. The present (i.e., of the period before the Second World War) also illuminates the past, for Mann's hero, F. D. Roosevelt, fulfils the role of this Joseph as politician, administrator, and sustainer. Joseph and Roosevelt pinpoint the extraordinary nature of a faith which turns the dreamer and his dreams into the servant who works through his dreams. Thus the abstract patterns of a timeless mythology interact in the contemporary story.

The length and complexity of the reborn myths answer to our modern needs. One may at first feel repelled by the thousand pages of Mann's *Joseph* when contrasted with the sparse economy of the book of Genesis. But the fluidity of our personal relationships has broken the dams of the ancient streams. The modern Jacob, alas, has accumulated too many memories to allow himself to be squeezed into fewer lines. Moreover, his inward struggle is even more complex than his war with external enemies. The range of Joseph's fantasies demands a great deal of space. But the substance remains unchanged. The modern patriarchs still have their Mount Moriah, Bethel, Penuel, and hunt, steal, harass, cheat and are cheated, fight and are lamed, love and suffer bereavement, and thus in the endless vicissitudes of fatherhood, sonship, brotherhood, and marriage, encounter the Other, the Ground of all being, the God of the Fathers.

This confrontation with the Other does not occur in a vacuum but in the strained relationships with other humans. It reaches its peak in the polarity of man and woman. The ancient Adam-Eve duality serves here only as a model, for in modern literature the 'eternal feminine' is as ambiguous as the volatile male. They no longer resemble the draped women of Greek sculpture, nor do they exhibit the steady character of the women of the biblical tradition. In the Scriptures the women are mostly 'good', and even if they suffer, like Naomi and Ruth, they do not really change. Even a defiant queen, like Jezebel, remains true to herself. But modern woman, like man, is lost in the general fragmentation of society and inner ambiguity. Hence even the war between the sexes can no longer be mirrored as in the conventional novels of the last century, when rank and property played an even greater part than fidelity. Now the status of bride and wife has become as questionable as that of Virgin and Mother. The principle of correspondence no longer operates to link a Beatrice to Mary, or even a Gretchen to the redeemed penitent, or a Solveig to the romantic ideal.

The man-woman confrontation recalls rather the demonic ladies of the past, such as Clytemnestra, Electra, Antigone, Penthesilea, sinned against and sinning. The unsatisfied and seductive, such as Potiphar's wife, and the obsessively murderous, like Salome and Herodias, effect the course of events in modern literature. Proust's long line of girls and women —Odette, Gilberte, Albertine—become corrupt in their reaction to a corrupt world. Kafka's women always attract men to leave them disappointed and exhausted. For example, K.'s Frieda, whose name conveys peace (Friede), after a brief affair and engagement, suspects K. and abandons him. She could have saved him, but she pushes him further into desolation. Thomas Mann's women, too, embody a demonic potential for good which they either cannot or will not bring to fruition. The group around Dr Faustus contribute to the general air of frigidity. They can mourn, but they cannot save, for they do not love. Indeed, ordinary family love simply no longer functions. Mann's Joseph, though married with children (as in Genesis), finds fulfilment outside (as, indeed, F. D. Roosevelt!). The modern story yields not only a crop of adulteries, separations, and even murders and suicides, but a belief that Eros is the god who attracts to deceive, and that the love which unites man and woman destroys both.

This pessimism restates the themes of the fall and the expulsion from Paradise. Desire, which is the mainspring of all action, releases a demonic force. But this force is not wholly negative, but can, through the story, release the positive. The crisis is inevitable. The conversion of the destructive hatred into healing acceptance between man and woman acts as the pivot of an acceptance on a larger scale. The divine comedy is still enacted when the recesses of neurotic behaviour are opened to the vastness of the cosmos. The dying K. may not be redeemed, but, according to Kafka's unwritten intentions, is accepted, not in answer to his striving, but because of certain 'auxiliary circumstances'. The regaining of Paradise, then, lies outside the logic of the story and is not the consequence of Jack and Jill being united after all the troubles. Contemporary writers look for the extraordinary, beyond routine and endeavour. The broken human relationships press on towards the apocalyptic.

The modern story finds its own level of apocalyptic. The ancient images are still present, though transformed. The woes, the seven seals, the attacks of dragon and beasts, spring up no longer from outside, but from within. The riders of the horses still herald war, famine, pestilence, and death to a suffering world, for, as Patrick White shows so movingly, *The Riders of the Chariot* trample the souls in modern Australia as in antiquity. In the full-length saga, where men and women do battle, witches, soothsayers, sorcerers, magicians, idolaters operate from within the system. The enemies, whom Deuteronomy outlaws and Luke denounces, cannot be got rid of. The victory of the Lamb over the dragon remains in question.

Modern literature portrays the divine-demonic split in human society in apocalyptic colours, but the modern apocalypse often fails to mediate new life. It often purges us with pity and terror, but it does not make good our escape from hell. Unless our chemical mutations beckon to a beyond we are doomed to an apocalyptic cycle which reveals nothing. This nothing is hell. Alexander Solzhenitsyn is the contemporary Dante who opens *The First Circle*, the threshold of deeper and deeper hells. In the company of 'privileged' prisoners we not only endure all the pains of our lot in a demonic system, but anticipate the way of escape. The first circle reveals, on the one hand, the threat of many circles, deeper yet and more frightful, to which the orbits of our society correspond. On the other it discloses the face-to-face encounter with absurdities, treacheries, frustrations, and cruelties. Heroic resolution of personal goodness overcomes the computerized nothingness. The lamb is slain and conquers.

This revelation comes in our recognition that 'it is so'. The moment of this *anagnorisis* may be filled with ecstatic laughter or with tragic sadness. It is a surprise, by joy or desolation. Prince Andrew in *War and Peace*, wounded and racked with pain near the battlefield of Austerlitz after the roar of the guns has moved on, speaks for many: 'I know now'. He had always known, in effect, but he had not recognized what he had known. Now the clouds, trailing over the blue sky, and the pain, trigger off the taste for the transcendent and abiding. It is not yet faith, but a prelude to it. The experience converges upon the not-yet, not-here. Gradually the Face of the Other is apprehended, reflected in the many known appearances and familiar circumstances. The Face of the One shines like crystal in and through the events and the conflict of human beings.

The moment of recognition may be succeeded by a constant and deepening response. It depends largely upon the use we make of the story. The ancient scriptures had their effect by ritualistic recitals. In our world the art of re-reading can achieve the same miracle. The transforming power of words seems to be controlled by our will to come to them again and again. They contrast sharply with the games we watch or the casual intercourse we have with acquaintances. The narrative assumes an authority of its own when it is released from the pages of the book.

This authority, unlike philosophy, does not depend upon abstractions and generalizations. The details, brought to verbal perfection, possess an authenticity of their own. In the biblical stories land, water, animals, birds, fish, the land, sea, and stars, are the primary materials from which the whole portrayal of reality proceeds. The modern story spirals in ever-widening circles and with ever-increasing concentration over and against the canvas. The human conflict in its grim realism is the point of contact and of confrontation with God.

This faith is made by identification with the conflict and sustained by the hope which lies beyond its resolution. The story provides the link. As it entertains and delights, shocks and warns, accuses and challenges, separates and unifies, imprisons and liberates, it reveals us to ourselves, evokes the dimensions of the universe behind ours, and points to the One, always absent and present, immutably transcendent and compassionately with us. We know nothing directly of salvation, peace, resurrection, and eternal life, but the Spirit addresses man to embrace the future in hope. This is the Spirit which moves men to a faith greater than the story itself, for as the story-teller talks and writes, and as the reader listens and reads, God himself confronts both for the future.

Select Bibliography

Standard encyclopaedias, dictionaries, introductions, and commentaries on biblical literature are listed under the following Library of Congress Classification:

BL   BR   BS   BT

and general background under DS

The Cambridge History of the Bible, Vol. 1, 1970.

Grant, M., *The Ancient Historians*, 1970.

Gerhardsson, B., *Memory and manuscript*, 1961.

Henn, T. R., *The Bible as literature*, 1970.

Palmer, H., *The Logic of Gospel Criticism*, 1968.

Schökel, L. A., *The Inspired Word*, 1965.

Toynbee, A., ed., *The Crucible of Christianity*, 1969.

Westermann, C., ed., *Essays on Old Testament Interpretation*, 1963.

Chapter 2

Galanopolous, A. G. & Bacon E., *Atlantis: the Truth behind the Legend*, 1969.

Gordon, C. H., *The Common Background of Greek and Hebrew Civilisation*, 1965.

Guthrie, W. K. C., *The Greeks and the gods*, 1968.

Kirk, G. S., *Myth*, 1970.

Webster, T. B. L., *From Mycenae to Homer*, 1964.

Wright, G. E., *ed., The Bible and the Ancient Near East: Essays in honour of W. F. Albright*, 1961.

Chapter 3

Habel, N. C., *Yahweh versus Baal*, 1964.

Oldenburg, U., *The Conflict between El and Ba'al in Canaanite Religion*, 1969.

von Rad, G., *The Problem of the Hexateuch and other Essays*, 1965; esp. chs. 8 and 15.

Chapter 4
Long, B. O., *The Problem of the Etiological Narrative in the Old Testament*, 1968.
von Rad, G., *Genesis*, 1961.

Chapter 5
Redford, D. B., *A Study of the Biblical Story of Joseph*, 1970.

Chapter 6
Auerbach, E., *Moses*, 1953.
Buber, M., *Moses*, 1946.
Thomson, R. J., *Moses and the Law in a Century of Criticism since Graf*, 1970.

Chapter 7
Carlson, R. A., *David the Chosen King*, 1964.
Whybray, R. N., *The Succession Narrative*, 1968.

Chapter 8
Bronner, L., *The Stories of Elijah and Elisha*, 1968.
Steck, O. H., *Überlieferung und Zeitgeschichte in den Elia Erzählungen*, 1968.

Chapter 9
Wijngaards, J. N. M., *The dramatization of Salvific History in the Deuteronomic Schools*, 1969.

Chapter 10
Eichrodt, W., *Theology of the Old Testament*, Pt II, 1967.

Chapter 11
Ackroyd, P. R., *The Age of the Chronicler*, 1970.

Chapters 12–14
Russell, D. S., *The Method and Message of Jewish Apocalyptic*, 1964.

Vermes, G., *Scripture and Tradition*, 1961.

Chapter 15
Black, M., *An Aramaic Approach to the Gospels and Acts*, 1967.
Derrett, I. D. M., *Law in the New Testament*, 1970; esp. ch. 17.
Jeremias, J., *Jerusalem at the time of Jesus*, 1969.
    New Testament Theology, 1971—
Käsemann, E., *New Testament Questions of Today*, 1969.

Chapter 16
Meeks, W. A., *The Prophet King*, 1967.
Smith, D. M., Jr., *The Composition and Order of the Fourth Gospel*, 1965.

Chapter 17
Bowman, J., *The Gospel of Mark*, 1965.
Brandon, S. G. F., *The Fall of Jerusalem*, 1951.
    Jesus and the Zealots, 1967.
Haenchen, E., *Der Weg Jesu*, 1968.
Jeremias, J., *The Parables of Jesus*, 1963.
Marxsen, W., *Mark the Evangelist*, 1969.
Moule, C. F. D., ed., *Miracles*, 1965.
Wilder, Amos N., *Eschatology and the Speech Modes of the Gospel*, in *Zeit und Geschichte* (Bultmann *Festschrift*), 1964.

Chapter 18
Davies, W. D., *The Setting of the Sermon on the Mount*, 1964.
Stendahl, K., *School of St Matthew*, 1968.

Chapter 19
Conzelmann, H., *Die Apostelgeschichte*, 1963.
Ehrhardt, A., *The Framework and Purpose of the Acts of the Apostles*, 1964.
Keck, L. E., and Martyn, J. L., ed., *Studies in Luke-Acts*, 1968.
Marshall, I. H., *Recent Study of Luke Acts*, Expository Times 80.

Chapter 20
Daube, D., *He that Cometh*, 1966.
Glatzer, N. N., ed., *The Passover Haggadah*, 1969.

Jeremias, J., *The Eucharistic Words of Jesus*, 1966.
Roth, C., *The Haggadah*, 1959.
S.P.C.K. Theological Collections:
9. *Eucharistic Theology Then and Now*, 1968.
10. *Word and Sacrament*, 1968.

Chapter 21
Cambridge History of the Bible, Vols. 2 (1969) and 3 (1963).
Metzger, B. M., *Index to Periodical Literature on Christ and the Gospels*, 1966, pp. 538-45.
Terselle, S. M., *Literature and the Christian Life*, 1966.

Chapter 22
Berlin, Isaiah, *The Hedgehog and the Fox*, 1953.
Chadwick, H. M. and N. K., *The Growth of Literature*, Vol. 2, 1936.
Collingwood, R. G., *The Principle of Art*, 1955.
Crews, F. C., *The Pooh Perplex*, 1953.
Frye, Northrop, *Anatomy of Criticism*, 1957.
Gibson, A. Boyce, *The Religion of Dostoevsky*, 1973.
Hildick, W., *Thirteen Types of Narrative*, 1968.
Killinger, J., *The Failure of Theology in Modern Literature*, 1963.
Lonergan, B., *Insight*, 1957; esp. ch. 17.
Sypher, W., *Four Stages of Renaissance Style*, 1955.
Ziolkowski, T., *Fictional Transfigurations of Jesus*, 1972.

Chapter 23
Auerbach, E., *Mimesis*, 1945.
Balthasar, H. U. von, *Herrlichkeit*, 3 vols., 1961-5.
Charity, A. C., *Events and their afterlife*, 1966.
Emrich, W., *Franz Kafka*, N.Y. 1968.
Gardner, H., *Religion and Literature*, 1971.
Gray, R., *Kafka's Castle*, 1956.
Hatfield, H., ed., *Thomas Mann, A collection of critical essays*, 1964.
Heller, E., *The Ironic German*, a study of Thomas Mann, 1958.

Henning, M., *Die Ich-Form und ihre Funktion in Thomas Manns Doktor Faustus*, 1966.

20th century Interpretations of the Castle; ed. Peter F Neumeyer, N.J. 1969.